best practices in faculty evaluation

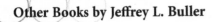

Other Books by Jeffrey L. Buller

Academic Leadership Day By Day: Small Steps That Lead to Great Success

The Essential Department Chair: A Comprehensive Desk Reference, Second Edition

The Essential Academic Dean: A Practical Guide to College Leadership

The Essential College Professor: A Practical Guide to an Academic Career

Classically Romantic: Classical Form and Meaning in Wagner's Ring

best practices

in faculty

evaluation

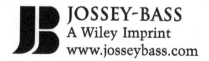

a practical guide for
academic leaders

jeffrey l. buller

JOSSEY-BASS
A Wiley Imprint
www.josseybass.com

Published by Jossey-Bass
A Wiley Imprint
One Montgomery Street, Suite 1200, San Francisco, CA 94104-4594—www.josseybass.com

Jossey-Bass books and products are available through most bookstores. To contact Jossey-Bass directly call our Customer Care Department within the U.S. at 800-956-7739, outside the U.S. at 317-572-3986, or fax 317-572-4002.

Wiley publishes in a variety of print and electronic formats and by print-on-demand. Some material included with standard print versions of this book may not be included in e-books or in print-on-demand. If this book refers to media such as a CD or DVD that is not included in the version you purchased, you may download this material at **http://booksupport.wiley.com**. For more information about Wiley products, visit **www.wiley.com**.

Library of Congress Cataloging-in-Publication Data
Buller, Jeffrey L.
    Best practices in faculty evaluation : a practical guide for academic leaders / Jeffrey L. Buller.
– First edition.
        pages cm
    Includes bibliographical references and index.
    ISBN 978-1-118-11843-6; ISBN 978-1-118-22451-9 (ebk); ISBN 978-1-118-23788-5 (ebk);
ISBN 978-1-118-26268-9 (ebk)
    1. College teachers–Rating of–United States.   2. Universities and colleges–United States–
Evaluation.   I. Title.
    LB2333.B85 2012
    378.1'2–dc23

                                2012016816

Printed in the United States of America
FIRST EDITION
HB Printing   10 9 8 7 6 5 4 3

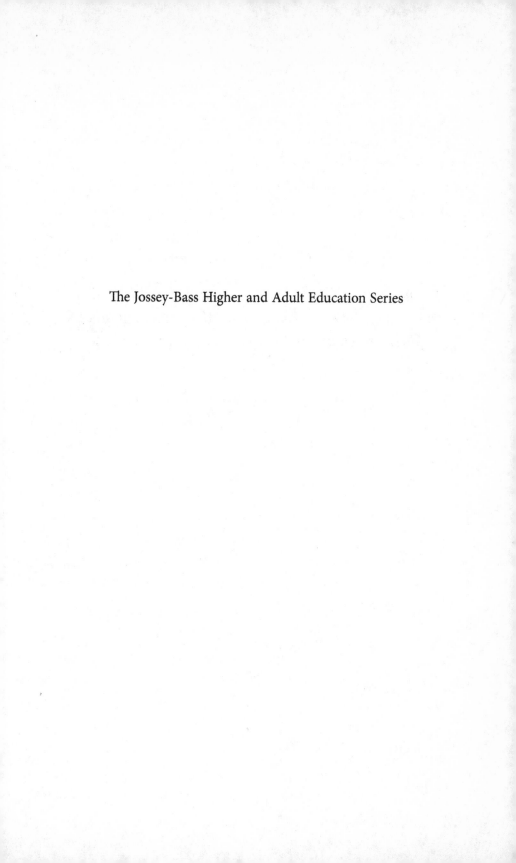

The Jossey-Bass Higher and Adult Education Series

For Raoul Arreola, Peter Seldin, and the countless other scholars who have worked to make the evaluation process fairer, easier, and more useful for faculty members

contents

viii   contents

the author

Jeffrey L. Buller is dean of the Harriet L. Wilkes Honors College of Florida Atlantic University. He began his administrative career as honors director and chair of the Department of Classical Studies at Loras College in Dubuque, Iowa, before going on to assume a number of administrative appointments at Georgia Southern University and Mary Baldwin College.

Buller is the author of *The Essential Department Chair: A Comprehensive Desk* Reference (2012), *Academic Leadership Day by Day: Small Steps That Lead to Great Success* (Jossey-Bass, 2011), *The Essential College Professor: A Practical Guide to an Academic Career* (Jossey-Bass, 2010), *The Essential Academic Dean: A Practical Guide to College Leadership* (Jossey-Bass, 2007), and *Classically Romantic: Classical Form and Meaning in Wagner's Ring* (Xlibris, 2001). He has also written numerous articles on Greek and Latin literature, nineteenth- and twentieth-century opera, and college administration.

From 2003 to 2005, Buller served as the principal English-language lecturer at the International Wagner Festival in Bayreuth, Germany. More recently, he has been active as a consultant to Sistema Universitario Ana G. Méndez in Puerto Rico and the Ministry of Higher Education in Saudi Arabia, where he is assisting with the creation of a kingdom-wide academic leadership center.

introduction and acknowledgments

At first glance, it may seem as if faculty reviews and evaluations pose no difficulty whatsoever for the members of the administration and faculty who conduct them. After all, professionals in higher education review and evaluate students all the time. We assess our academic programs. We review research in our disciplines. And we've all been reviewed and evaluated ourselves. So how hard can it possibly be to apply those same skills to evaluations of our faculty? The answer, as you know or you wouldn't be reading this book, is, "Very hard indeed." Those other processes are very limited when it comes to borrowing from them for the evaluation of a colleague. For one thing, he or she *is* a colleague. No matter whether you're the chancellor of a university system or an adjunct instructor of a single course, the concepts of collegiality, shared governance, and academic freedom probably resonate very strongly for you. In other words, every faculty evaluation is, in some ways, the evaluation of a peer, and just as you would object to someone who criticized your teaching techniques or research methods simply because they were different from his or her own, you may find it challenging at times to draw the line between upholding standards, offering advice, and meddling inappropriately. It can feel very awkward to be in a position of judging someone who in other situations is on your same level as a colleague—and who may someday be evaluating you.

Second, so many aspects of faculty reviews and evaluations seem rather subjective. What distinguishes "good" from "excellent" teaching, research, and service? How do you know whether someone's instruction is really effective without relying too much on student ratings of instruction? How many peer-reviewed articles is "enough" when you're looking at a relatively short period of time, as you do during an annual review? Should service on a major institutional committee count as much as serving as an officer in a professional association? Should it count more? Less? When it comes to faculty reviews and evaluations, you can become immobilized just by trying to answer these basic questions.

Best Practices in Faculty Evaluation will provide you with the information and skills you'll need in order to perform these tasks more fairly, easily, and confidently. Most books dealing with reviews focus on the evaluation procedure itself. They're wonderful resources if you're looking to develop a new policy for conducting evaluations in your discipline or at your school, but they provide little help to you if there's a system already in place and you just want to become a better reviewer. This book is a guide to doing exactly that: a training manual for administrators who want to become more effective and less anxious when they're evaluating someone. Even when I am discussing a specific evaluation procedure, I offer ideas about how you can borrow certain aspects of that procedure and apply them to whatever system your school happens to be using. At every point, I've tried to take my subtitle—*A Practical Guide for Academic Leaders*—literally, offering advice to those who have never conducted a review before, as well as those who have had decades of experience but still want to learn more. I've tried to keep the emphasis on what you need to know immediately if there's a stack of portfolios on your desk right now that you have to review by the end of the week. My goal, in short, is to be as practical as possible in as concrete a manner as possible. It's the information I wish I'd had when, as a newly appointed department chair at age twenty-seven, I had to conduct my first annual evaluations, and the other members of my department were all full professors, aged sixty-seven, sixty-eight, and seventy-two, respectively. Did I mention that they'd be voting on my tenure in a few years? Taking the job seriously and not endangering my own future required a delicate balancing act, and I would have loved a little advice on what to do.

Some chapters, such as those on tenure and posttenure reviews, have necessarily been written from the viewpoint of evaluating the typical full-time, tenure-eligible faculty member. But that faculty member is often no longer typical. Increasing numbers of part-time faculty members, non-tenure-track faculty members, and even online course instructors whom the reviewer never meets in person are on the staff of most colleges and universities. For that reason, I have tried to avoid the underlying assumption that every evaluation for promotion to the rank of associate professor is inevitably also a tenure evaluation or that every annual review of an untenured faculty member is also a probationary pretenure review. I have separated these topics into different chapters, even though they are often single processes at some institutions. If your interest is primarily in evaluating faculty members who are not eligible for tenure, you may wish to focus your attention on Chapters Two through Four, Seven, and Nine through Twelve, which I wrote with these concerns specifically in mind.

Even experienced chairs, deans, and vice presidents can feel a good deal of anxiety when they approach faculty reviews and evaluations. It may be impossible to make this task enjoyable or completely anxiety free, but it is possible to make it a little bit easier, less likely to result in appeals or grievances, and more beneficial to the discipline, institution, and faculty member under review, all at the same time.

As you read through the chapters in this book, consider discussing various ideas and suggestions with your peers. How do they approach evaluations in their areas? Which recommendations do they think will be most effective in your own evaluation environment? How can you continue to develop your skills as a reviewer each year that evaluation is your responsibility? These are some of the questions you might consider as you work through these issues with your colleagues. How to conduct faculty reviews also is a good topic for a faculty development or administrative leadership program, and this book can provide a basis for how to structure that type of training. Finally, it could be a valuable resource for new deans, department chairs, and chairs of promotion and tenure committees so that their job will be somewhat less stressful.

Beginning with Chapter Three, you'll find that most chapters contain a number of mini-case studies, designed to give you practice in the principles discussed in the chapter. But don't go looking for the right answers in the back of the book! There *are* no "right" answers to these problems, since your school will have its own set of policies and you'll have your own administrative style. So approach the mini-case studies not as riddles to be solved, but as complexities similar to those we face each day as academic leaders.

○ acknowledgments

Throughout the preparation of this book, I've owed a large debt of gratitude to our office's student intern, Megan Geiger, who has cheerfully typed many of the quotations that appear in each chapter, tracked down sources, and provided an expert proofreading eye. I'm also grateful to all the institutions and organizations for which I've provided workshops on faculty evaluation for helping me to focus this topic through their questions and comments. The three anonymous reviewers of this book provided valuable suggestions that greatly helped me improve its content. Finally, I thank Sheryl Fullerton and the rest of the editorial staff at Jossey-Bass for their continued support and encouragement. If I were reviewing any of you, I'd be sure to give you my highest recommendation.

Jeffrey L. Buller

Jupiter, Florida
June 1, 2012

part one

the fundamental goals of review and evaluation

1

the accountability culture in higher education

For much of the history of higher education, conducting student or faculty surveys—even conducting formal student examinations—was relatively rare. In some systems, course examinations either didn't occur at all or didn't play a major role in a student's progress; the important test was the set of comprehensive examinations that occurred just before the granting of a degree. (See, for example, Amano, 1990; Kehm, 2001; Wiseman, 1961; Min and Xiuwen, 2001.) Even well into the twentieth century at American universities, many courses based a student's grade solely on a final examination or research paper (Smallwood, 1935). Some professors also gave a midterm exam, and some courses included quizzes or tests after each major unit, but the notion of frequent grading opportunities was not particularly common at most colleges and universities.

Even less common were student satisfaction surveys, forms evaluating professors or administrators, and structured performance reviews of staff members. The assumption was that the faculty knew far better than the students what needed to be taught in university-level courses, and administrators were responsible for making sure that the faculty taught those courses effectively. They may not have

evaluated those faculty members in a regular and former manner, but
if they gained some sense that a particular instructor was ineffective,
they responded with either advice or termination of the person's contract. Systematic efforts to assess the effectiveness of academic programs
or evaluate the continual improvement in a faculty member's teaching,
research, and service were all but unknown. And then, seemingly all at
once, everything seemed to change.

o   why everyone always seems to be evaluating everyone else

If you enter a university in many parts of the world today, you're likely
to encounter a bewildering array of surveys, assessment instruments,
and examinations. Whatever can be studied for its effectiveness and
ability to improve *is* studied, sometimes in multiple competing ways.
Here is just a sample of some of the reviews, appraisals, analyses, and
studies that are commonplace in higher education today:

- Entering student surveys like the Cooperative Institutional Research
  Program's Freshman Survey, administered by the Higher Education
  Research Institute at UCLA
- Surveys by institutional admissions offices about why students did
  or did not choose to attend that school
- Course quizzes and tests, including final exams
- Comprehensive examinations for degrees
- Licensure exams
- Self-studies, compliance reports, and inventories for institutional
  accreditation
- Self-studies, compliance reports, and inventories for specialized
  accreditation in individual disciplines
- Course evaluations completed by students
- Course evaluations completed by faculty peers or administrators
- Administrator evaluations completed by faculty members, peers,
  and supervisors

- Staff performance appraisals
- Assessment reports on the effectiveness of the general education program, individual degree programs, and each office or unit on campus
- Comprehensive program reviews to gauge the quality, sustainability, and centrality to mission of various degree programs and campus offices
- Student satisfaction surveys
- Graduating student surveys
- Employee surveys
- Morale studies
- Alumni surveys

Add to these the countless Web sites on which reviews of instructors appear, such as ratemyprofessors.com, rateyourprof.com, ProfessorPerformance.com, and myedu.com. And given enough time, we might come up with several dozen other ways in which professors, academic programs, and institutions are continually reviewed, ranked, surveyed, studied, and assessed. In one sense, it can be misleading to lump very different items together, as I've done in the above list, perhaps leading to the danger of false comparisons. But in another sense, each item represents one important way in which higher education or its critics investigate what people know, how people feel, or what people believe about higher education, all in an effort to determine how well something or someone has performed.

The truly interesting thing is that most of these reviews and studies are relatively new. Colleges and universities seemed to get along without them rather well for centuries, but then, starting in the late 1960s and early 1970s, the use of surveys, inventories, multiple examinations in a course, and personnel reviews began to multiply rapidly. And no matter how different some of us may consider these processes to be, people do tend to confuse them. It's not at all uncommon for faculty members to ask, "Why do we have to do assessment? We already assess our students in class every time we determine their grades," or "Why do we have to do program review? We already do assessment." In other words, if we really want to get the information we need in order to draw informed conclusions, avoid unnecessary duplication of effort, and improve both our own performance and the effectiveness of our academic programs, we need to understand three things:

1. Exactly what each type of review or evaluation can and can't tell us
2. How to interpret the information gained from that type of review or evaluation
3. Why gathering all that information is important to improvement of our programs and personnel

To obtain that understanding, we have to begin this discussion of faculty reviews and evaluations with a brief history of where all these different processes came from and why they seem to have multiplied so suddenly. The question to ask, therefore, is, "Why in higher education today does everyone always seem to be evaluating everyone else?"

Three trends in American higher education emerged during the 1960s and 1970s that coalesced into what we might term today's accountability culture in higher education:

1. *The desire of universities to increase their retention rates and levels of student success began causing professors to move away from basing grades largely on a single major project or exam and to introduce multiple grading opportunities throughout their courses.* As the population of colleges and universities expanded and diversified in the 1950s and 1960s due to the GI Bill and the civil rights movement, many faculty members felt a need to give students earlier feedback about their progress in a course so that they could take action to get back on track, if necessary, before it was too late. Particularly before military conscription effectively ended in the United States in 1973, failing out of college could cause a student to end up being drafted to fight in a highly unpopular war or, at least, to be faced with relatively few options for a desirable career. As a result, higher education made a slow but

perceptible shift from seeing itself as the touchstone that determined who would and who would not graduate to becoming the "student-friendly" or "student-centered" environment familiar at colleges and universities today.

2. *A new theoretical model gave institutions a mechanism for measuring their impact and thus demonstrating to parents, donors, and potential students the benefits that they provided.* Trudy Banta (2002), perhaps the nation's leading expert on assessment and its role in American higher education, credits four major works that emerged between 1969 and 1980 with laying the groundwork for today's culture of academic of academic accountability. First, Kenneth Feldman and Theodore Newcomb's two-volume *The Impact of College on Students* (1969) brought together four decades of research measuring the impact that higher education has on the lives of traditional-aged college students, the type of maturation these students experience during their college years, and the significant role this research could play at the universities of the future. Second, Alexander Astin's *Four Critical Years* (1977) established the metaphor of "value-added" approaches and promoted the use of longitudinal studies to examine net effects. Third, Howard Bowen's *Investment in Learning* (1977) helped establish a public policy context for assessment by emphasizing the societal returns on investment associated with higher education. And, fourth, Robert Pace's *Measuring Outcomes of College* (1979) emphasized the role of college environments and actual student behaviors. Together these works provided higher education with both a conceptual framework for assessment—the goal of college teaching is to improve student learning in mastery of the course's content, critical thinking, and effective communication—and a methodology—the setting and measuring of learning outcomes—that scholars could use to document what a university actually does for students and how effective it is in achieving those goals. Since researchers often act on the principle that if something can be studied, it soon will be studied, it wasn't long before investigations into the measurable impact of higher education began in earnest.

3. *As the costs of higher education rose despite frequent downturns in the economy, legislators and others who paid the bills for college education began to ask for objective data about their return on investment.* Concurrently with the first two trends, the cost of receiving an education at an American college or university climbed significantly. According to the *Congressional Record* of April 10, 2000, the Senate found that "the cost of attaining a higher education has outpaced both inflation and median family incomes. Specifically, over the past 20 years, the cost of college tuition has quadrupled (growing faster than any consumer item, including health care and nearly twice as fast as inflation) and 8 times as fast as median household income. . . . According to the Department of Education, there is approximately $150,000,000,000 in outstanding student loan debt, and students borrowed more during the 1990s than during the 1960s, 1970s and 1980s combined" (Title I, 2000, p. 5051). Not surprisingly, the number of articles, editorials, and legislative inquiries into the return—frequently in the sense of the economic return—on this investment began to soar as one century ended and the next got under way. Here's how an analysis by the Education Resources Information Center described the situation in 2002:

> The escalating cost of higher education is causing many to question the value of continuing education beyond high school. Many wonder whether the high cost of tuition, the opportunity cost of choosing college over full-time employment, and the accumulation of thousands of dollars of debt is, in the long run, worth the investment. The risk is especially large for low-income families who have a difficult time making ends meet without the additional burden of college tuition and fees. . . . While it is clear that investment in a college degree, especially for those students in the lowest income brackets, is a financial burden, the long-term benefits to individuals as well as to society at large, appear to far outweigh the costs [Porter 2002].

In a similar way, the College Board released a study, *College Pays 2010: The Benefits of Higher Education for Individuals and Society, in Brief* (2010), that documented the difference in median income between workers with or without a bachelor's degree, the positive effect that universities have on the tax revenues of states and communities, the decreased medical costs incurred by the college educated because of their healthier lifestyles, and so on (Baum, Ma, and Payea, 2010). At the same time, exposés such as Richard Arum and Josipa Roksa's *Academically Adrift* (2011), Andrew Hacker and Claudia Dreifus's *Higher Education?* (2010), Marc Scheer's *No Sucker Left Behind* (2008), and Craig Brandon's *The Five-Year Party* (2010) helped make the public increasingly skeptical that colleges and universities were actually worth their high expense. Internal studies, reviews, and evaluations thus became a way for institutions to document that higher education does indeed make a positive difference in the lives of students and the welfare of the community. Assessment reports and staff evaluations were used to illustrate that colleges were continually focused on improving the quality of their programs, achieving the goals in student learning they claimed to be achieving, and holding faculty members to a very high standard.

Not coincidentally, a lack of public confidence in the quality of American primary and secondary education led to a call for more frequent standardized testing at all levels of instruction. The No Child Left Behind Act of 2001, the Race to the Top Program of 2009 (with its emphasis on uniform standards and assessments), and the frequent demand that teachers' salaries be tied to student achievement have meant that by the time students reach college, they've spent two-thirds of their lives associating education with completing exams, surveys, evaluations, and all other types of assessment instruments as a regular part of the pedagogical process.

Public concern has exacerbated the already growing tendency to test college students more frequently, assess programs more thoroughly, evaluate faculty members more consistently, and review the effectiveness of administrators more rigorously. As a result, it's the rare university today that doesn't have an elaborate set of evaluation procedures and a formal office of institutional research or program effectiveness and assessment. Faculty members today thus have far greater responsibility for demonstrating to others the benefits of their programs than at any time before the late 1970s. Reviews, evaluations, appraisals, and assessments have become the familiar tools of the accountability culture that pervades American higher education in the twenty-first century. (For more insight into this topic, Larry Braskamp and John Ory, 1994, provide an overview of the factors that brought about regular faculty evaluation in America.)

o the significance of the accountability culture for reviewers

These background considerations lead us to a major question: While such explanations of why higher education has become so obsessed with evaluation and accountability may have some historical interest, what relevance do they have to a professor or administrator who simply wants to know how best to conduct a faculty review? Or, to put it another way, how does chronicling trends in higher education help anyone become a better evaluator? The answers to these questions may be found in the following principle that will guide us throughout this book:

> You can't review anything or anyone effectively unless you thoroughly under-stand what you're reviewing, why you're reviewing it, and how the results of your review will be used

In other words, because of the way in which the accountability culture developed in higher education, many different types of appraisals occur simultaneously. These different processes stem from a similar desire but serve very distinct purposes and, as we'll see, the way in which data are collected and analyzed for one of these purposes may make it inappropriate or even impossible to use those data for some other purpose. Why is this so? In order to answer this question, we need to continue our investigation by considering a brief primer on the processes that are used to collect information related to the quality of higher education.

The Differences Among Diagnostic, Formative, Summative, and Formative-Summative Processes

One of the key differences among types of review procedures stems from the various purposes for which data are being collected.

Diagnostic processes are designed to gather baseline data about a current situation and, in some instances, to provide insights into the best plan for proceeding in the future. In higher education, a foreign language placement test that determines into which level of study a student should be placed is a familiar diagnostic instrument. SWOT analysis—the identification of an organization's internal strengths and weaknesses, along with its external opportunities and threats—is a diagnostic procedure commonly used in the corporate world, as are inventories that determine the current effectiveness of an existing organizational structure before any modification is implemented.

Formative processes are those that yield constructive advice on how a procedure or performance can be improved. When faculty members survey their students early in a course to determine which pedagogical methods are working well and which need to be improved, they're engaging in a formative process. The students aren't graded on the basis of their answers, and the professor is neither rewarded nor penalized on the basis of what students say; the information merely provides guidance into how to make the class better.

Summative processes are those that result in a conclusive judgment. Assigning students a grade in a course is a summative process, as are promotion and tenure evaluations, academic program reviews, and hiring decisions. At the end of all these processes, a formal decision is made. The student either does or does not pass the course. The faculty member either is or is not promoted. The program is expanded, maintained, reduced, or eliminated. And so on. We might describe the difference by saying that reviewers act as coaches during formative processes; they act as judges during summative processes.

One of the most problematic areas of the faculty review and evaluation system occurs when a process is presented as formative but later
assumes a summative role (Manning, 1988). For instance, a class may
be told that student ratings of instruction are being administered only
to help faculty members improve their pedagogical methods, but results
from those instruments are later treated as documentation when the
faculty members come up for promotion. The problem with this change
isn't merely that the students were misled (although that's bad enough)
but also that people tend to respond differently to formative and summative processes. If a class is told, "We'd like to collect some information
about how to make this course better for you," the students may come
up with a far longer list of complaints and desired improvements than
if they're told, "We'd like to collect some information about whether this
faculty member will keep his or her job next year" (Stodolsky, 1984;
Spencer and Schmelkin, 2002).

When people are aware that an important decision about a person's
future will be made on the basis of their answers, they're more likely
to keep their criticism within certain limits than when they feel free to
speculate about what might constitute an ideal course. For this reason,
it's usually important to build a firewall between purely formative and
purely summative processes, giving administrators and review committees only information that was collected with the purpose clearly stated.
At many institutions, that division hasn't been kept, and this failure can
result in appeals, grievances, and even lawsuits after negative reviews.
For instance, a 2002 study by the Rutgers University Senate Faculty
Affairs and Personnel Committee found that a statement appearing on
that school's student course evaluation forms was misleading. With
regard to open-ended comments, the forms stated, "This information
is intended to be used by the instructor to modify or improve the
course," whereas these comments "have been used for personnel decisions in some departments" (senate.rutgers.edu/so109.html). Blurring
the distinction between formative and summative uses of evaluation in
this way could create a system in which negative personnel decisions
are successfully challenged. When the Rutgers Faculty Senate was

informed about the matter, they promptly removed the misleading statement from the forms.

Nevertheless, we saw a moment ago that "it's *usually* very important to build a firewall between formative and summative processes." There are times when combining these two types of review is either necessary or highly beneficial, although procedures need to be in place to make sure that no one completes an evaluation form under false pretenses. Steven Wininger (2005), professor of psychology at Western Kentucky University, has proposed an approach that he calls *formative-summative assessment* (FSA), which cycles back and forth between the two types of review without misusing the information gathered or misleading those who are involved in the process.

In his own work, Wininger adopted FSA primarily as a pedagogical tool for professors to use with students. For instance, in his educational psychology course, Winniger administers an exam for which students receive individual grades (summative), then uses the exam as a class-room exercise to improve skills where areas of understanding were low (formative), leading to a new grading opportunity (summative), and so on. In a faculty review setting, formative-summative evaluation could consist of conducting a formal evaluation procedure purely as a developmental exercise, with the stipulation that the results may not be considered during any later reviews, using the results of that procedure to develop a strategy to remediate any perceived areas of weakness, and then conducting the formal procedure again, this time in a summative manner, when a personnel decision (such as contract renewal, merit increase, or promotion) needs to be made.

In fact, in many systems, probationary pretenure reviews, which we'll consider in Chapter Five, are intended to function in precisely this way. The pretenure review provides the formative component of the process, while the actual tenure evaluation two or three years later provides the summative element. The complicating factor is, as we shall see, that faculty contracts are sometimes not renewed after particularly poor pretenure reviews. It's important, therefore, that the probationary faculty member who's undergoing pretenure review understand precisely what the possible results of the process may be. Otherwise even the best-intended formative-summative process could create problems for both the reviewer and the institution as an entity that failed to follow its own policies.

The Differences Among Review, Appraisal, Assessment, and Evaluation

The distinctions among diagnostic, formative, summative, and formative-summative reviews are important because they help to explain why higher education has developed so many processes that appear to gather very similar information. But there's also another reason for the multiplicity of these processes: due to the accountability culture in which higher education operates today, stakeholders want to verify that all parties involved in the academic enterprise are meeting the standards that have been set for them. The faculty and administration want to make sure that students have reached a certain level of performance before issuing a diploma. Accreditation bodies want to make sure that programs are adhering to certain requirements and guidelines before certifying them. Legislatures and governing boards want to make sure that institutions are using resources effectively before authorizing a new budget. Students and parents want to make sure that they're getting their money's worth. Because different types of conclusions need to be drawn by these different stakeholders, it's inadvisable—and frequently impossible—to make a single process that achieves all these purposes simultaneously. As a result, it's important for anyone involved in these processes to keep the terminology straight so as to avoid distorting the results or confusing the participants.

Although the terms are used with different meanings by other authors or in other situations, it's useful to clarify what these words are intended to mean in this book. For our purposes, a *review* is the most general term for any study that examines the performance of an individual or organization. We can thus refer to all processes we'll be considering—appraisals, evaluations, and assessments—generically as reviews. For this reason, every evaluation is a review, but not every review is an evaluation, and so on.

An *appraisal* is a type of review in which someone in a position of authority determines whether a person, unit, or program is meeting an established set of expectations. For example, in a performance appraisal, a supervisor rates an employee according to the degree to which he or she is handling the responsibilities detailed in that person's job description. In a program appraisal, the director or chair rates the degree to which a program is fulfilling its key objectives. In this way, appraisals always exist within a hierarchical reporting structure and involve comparisons between anticipated standards and actual performance. They're a much more focused type of review than some of the others we'll explore. In academic settings, it is most often administrators, staff members, and relatively small programs that undergo appraisals instead of other types of evaluation. Faculty members, complex programs, and the institution as a whole may undergo appraisals from time to time, but they are more frequently reviewed in other ways.

It is the difference between *assessment* and *evaluation* that tends to cause the greatest confusion on most college campuses. Perhaps the best way to understand the difference that I'll adopt in the chapters that follow is to consider how these processes diverge in three key areas (Buller, 2010, p. 88):

ASSESSMENT Is	EVALUATION Is
Formative; provides constructive advice on how an activity can be improved	Summative; renders a judgment as to whether a specific action is warranted
Process oriented; looks for ways to improve the activity itself	Goal oriented; determines whether a particular level of quality has been reached
Primarily concerned with larger or collective entities, such as an entire group of students in a course, courses in a curriculum, or departments in a college	Primarily concerned with individual entities, such as a single person, course, or program

Other books and systems use these terms in different ways—and you'll undoubtedly have your own preference—but for our purposes, I'll adhere to the distinctions I have outlined. They offer a convenient way of making some significant distinctions among various kinds of reviews. The key to these differences may best be seen by returning to the common faculty questions we encountered earlier: "Why do we have to do assessment? We already assess our students in class when we determine their grades." In light of the differences just outlined, grading a student in a course is an *evaluation*: it tells an observer how well that individual student did in meeting the course's pedagogical goals. In this manner, assigning a grade is summative: it renders a judgment about the level at which that student performed.

But student grades reveal nothing at all about the effectiveness of the course itself or how well that course has been integrated into an overall program of study. Those grades are influenced by too many other factors: each student's individual ability, how hard he or she studied, his or her familiarity with the material from previous courses, and so on. Moreover, nearly everyone in higher education is familiar with a situation in which the students of an introductory course all achieved very high grades but then performed poorly in later courses or on licensure exams. In this case, the students succeeded in the individual evaluations they'd received in their introductory courses—their tests, quizzes, papers, and assignments—but the curriculum as a whole hadn't been very effective in preparing those students for their later needs.

In order to gain a sense of how whole programs can be improved, colleges and university use *assessment*, an activity designed to improve the process of learning found in that program, not to rate the performance of individual students. The word *assessment* is derived from the Latin verb *assidere*, meaning to "sit beside." We can imagine assessment as what trusted counselors or mentors do when they sit with us, giving us the benefit of their guidance. *Evaluation* comes to English through the early French *evaluer*, which combined the Latin words *ex* (out of, from) and *valere* (to be strong, to have strengths) to denote the act of extracting something's merit from it or assigning it a value. Schools sometimes combine these two processes by embedding certain questions or types of problems into the exams of a particular course, but in this case, the intention of the two activities is different. The entire exam serves to evaluate each student; the same question on all the students' exams serves to assess the course. But no student's grade or even the average of all grades really tells you very much about how well a course has been designed or how effectively a professor has been teaching. Individual students may perform well, poorly, or somewhere in between in even the best-designed program, and any single student may excel in even the least effective program. You can't draw evaluation conclusions from assessment or vice versa.

○ why these differences matter when reviews are conducted

When we set out to conduct an actual review, the differences we've examined in the last two sections become very important. For example, if we don't distinguish carefully among evaluation, assessment, and appraisal, we can end up recommending unnecessary revisions to the curriculum when the problem is better addressed through faculty development or student remediation. Similarly, if we are careless in combining formative and summative processes, we could have our decisions overturned or find ourselves being sanctioned for failing to follow appropriate procedures. For this reason, we should begin every review process by making sure that we clearly understand the answers to the following questions:

1. What is the specific purpose of this review?
2. Who or what is being reviewed?
3. What are the possible outcomes of the review? In particular, what are the possible outcomes if the result of this review is strongly negative?
4. Is the person, unit, or program undergoing the review aware of these possible outcomes?

5. With whom will the results of the review be shared?

6. What sources of information am I required by institutional policy to consult as I conduct this review?

7. What sources of information am I allowed—even though not required—by institutional policy to consult as I conduct this review?

8. Are there strict deadlines I must meet in order for the results of my review to become valid?

9. What is the nature of my conclusion? Am I authorized to make a decision, or am I merely recommending a course of action to a supervisor, committee, or other party?

10. Does institutional policy require me to retain records of how I reached my decision for a certain period of time?

By understanding these issues before a review gets under way, we're less likely to collect or consider the type of information that doesn't really help us, make the type of mistakes that will invalidate our efforts, or have our own findings overturned on appeal or by higher administrative levels. In later chapters, we'll also consider other issues that should be considered for different types of reviews. But the central principle is always the same: *Unless you know precisely why you're conducting a review, you will have a very hard time identifying what to review and how to review it.*

o   why review and goal setting should be merged into a single, seamless process

Review by its very nature is a retrospective process. Even tenure reviews, which are intended to identify a faculty member's promise for the future, are based on a consideration of past achievements. But it's important that other types of review not become so focused on the past that they lose all sight of the future. Nearly every review should end with an agreement about specific goals for future development. It's easy to understand why goal setting would be important in formative evaluations. After all, the whole purpose of the process is to advise the person or program on ways to improve.

But why would goal setting be important for a summative process? Since these reviews culminate in a decision, what is the point of looking toward the future? The answer to these questions is that even summative processes don't imply that no further growth or achievement is possible. A faculty member who is promoted to the rank of associate professor still needs to earn promotion to the rank of full professor, and a faculty member who is promoted to the rank of full professor still needs to be successful in future posttenure reviews. A curriculum that receives universal praise during a program review will still be reviewed again in the future, and course content is always in a state of evolution and improvement as students change and knowledge expands. For this reason, review processes should conclude whenever possible with a discussion of what's next and the setting of future goals. These goals shouldn't restrict the person or program from taking advantage of unexpected new opportunities or modifying his or her plans as circumstances change. Nevertheless, the goals provide a general road map for further progress and a starting point for measuring that progress during future reviews.

You will notice that the language I have used is, "Review processes should conclude *whenever possible* with a discussion of what's next." When would it ever not be possible to merge reviews and goal setting into a single, seamless process? In certain systems, when a tenure decision is negative, the institution is forbidden to provide reasons for that decision. The rationale is that during a faculty member's probationary period, the institution is allowed to forgo renewing his or her annual contract for any reason or for no reason. In fact, the necessity for an institution to provide a reason for nonrenewal of contract is (along with the right of due process to challenge that decision) the very essence of what tenure guarantees. As a result, some systems consider it inappropriate to extend that right to an untenured faculty member who has failed a review by offering an explanation for the reasons behind the decision. (See, for example, Lander University, 2010; University of

Louisiana at Monroe, 2007; University of Tennessee, 1981.) Setting goals and developing plans for improvement with the faculty member could be construed as revealing why tenure was denied; looking toward the future thus unnecessarily clouds the true meaning of a negative tenure decision and opens the institution to a possible legal challenge. Since technically no justification is required, certain institutions conclude, no justification should ever be provided.

○ conclusion

A valuable source for emerging approaches to faculty review is *Assessment and Evaluation in Higher Education*, a peer-reviewed journal published seven times a year by Routledge. Known as *Assessment in Higher Education* until 1981, the journal's current title reflects its focus on both major types of review. Each issue contains eight to ten articles dealing with such issues as best practices in the use of student ratings, techniques for evaluating adjunct or distance learning faculty members, assessment techniques for measuring student progress in mastering new technologies, and so on. Since issues in higher education develop so rapidly, it's a good idea to supplement insights gained through books with an understanding of emerging trends, reported in such publications as the *Chronicle of Higher Education* and *Assessment and Evaluation in Higher Education*.

References
Amano, I. (1990). *Education and examination in modern Japan.* Tokyo: University of Tokyo Press.

Arum, R., & Roksa, J. (2011). *Academically adrift: Limited learning on college campuses.* Chicago: University of Chicago Press.

Astin, A. W. (1977). *Four critical years.* San Francisco: Jossey-Bass.

Banta, T. W. (2002). *Building a scholarship of assessment.* San Francisco: Jossey-Bass.

Baum, S., Ma, J., & Payea, K. (2010). *Education pays 2010: The benefits of higher education for individuals and society.* New York: College Board. Retrieved from trends.collegeboard.org/downloads/Education_Pays_2010.pdf.

Bowen, H. R. (1977). *Investment in learning: The individual and social value of American higher education*. San Francisco: Jossey-Bass.

Brandon, C. (2010). *The five-year party: How colleges have given up on educating your child and what you can do about it*. Dallas: BenBella.

Braskamp, L. A., & Ory, J. C. (1994). *Assessing faculty work: Enhancing individual and institutional performance*. San Francisco: Jossey-Bass.

Buller, J. L. (2010). *The essential college professor: A practical guide to an academic career*. San Francisco: Jossey-Bass.

College Board. (2010). *College pays 2010: The benefits of higher education for individuals and society, in brief*. New York: College Board. Retrieved from http://trends.collegeboard.org/downloads/Education_Pays_2010_In_Brief.pdf.

Feldman, K. A., & Newcomb, T. M. (1969). *The impact of college on students*. San Francisco: Jossey-Bass.

Hacker, A., & Dreifus, C. (2010). *Higher education? How colleges are wasting our money and failing our kids—and what we can do about it*. New York: Times Books.

Kehm, B. (2001, March). Oral examinations at German universities. *Assessment in Education: Principles, Policy and Practice, 8*(1), 25–31.

Lander University. (2010). *Faculty handbook*. Retrieved from www.lander.edu/Libraries/Site_Documents/Faculty_Handbook.sflb.ashx

Manning, R. C. (1988). *The teacher evaluation handbook: Step-by-step techniques and forms for improving instruction*. Upper Saddle River, NJ: Prentice Hall.

Min, H., & Xiuwen, Y. (2001, March). Educational assessment in China: Lessons from history and future prospects. *Assessment in Education: Principles, Policy and Practice, 8*(1), 5–10.

Pace, C. R. (1979). *Measuring outcomes of college: Fifty years of findings and recommendations for the future*. San Francisco: Jossey-Bass.

Porter, K. (2002). The value of a college degree. *ERIC Digest*. Washington, DC: ERIC Clearinghouse on Higher Education. (ERIC Document Reproduction Service No. ED470038). Retrieved from www.ericdigests.org/2003-3/value.htm

Scheer, M. (2008). *No sucker left behind: Avoiding the great college rip-off*. Monroe, ME: Common Courage Press.

Smallwood, M. L. (1935). *An historical study of examinations and grading systems in early American universities*. Cambridge, MA: Harvard University Press.

Spencer, K., & Schmelkin, L. P. (2002). Student perspectives on teaching and its evaluation. *Assessment and Evaluation in Higher Education, 27*, 397–409.

Stodolsky, S. S. (1984). Teacher evaluation: The limits of looking. *Educational Researcher, 13*(9), 11–18.

Title I: Levels and Amounts, Sec. 302. (2000, April 10). *Congressional Record, 146*, Pt. 4.

University of Louisiana at Monroe. (2007). *Faculty handbook*. Retrieved from www.ulm.edu/ncate/standard%205/Exhibits/5d1.1/FacultyHandbook.pdf.

University of Tennessee. (1981, May 25). *Faculty senate memorandum*. Retrieved from web.utk.edu/~senate/MemoReasonsDenial.html.

Wininger, S. R. (2005). Using your tests to teach: Formative summative assessment. *Teaching of Psychology, 32*, 164–166.

Wiseman, S. (1961). *Examinations and English education*. Manchester: Manchester University Press.

Resources

Buller, J. L. (2008). Why all evaluations aren't alike. *Academic Leader, 24*(12), 4–5.

Feldman, K. A. (2007). Identifying exemplary teachers and teaching: Evidence from student ratings. In R. P. Perry & J. C. Smart (Eds.), *The scholarship of teaching and learning in higher education: An evidence-based perspective*. Dordrecht: Springer.

Goldman, G. K., & Zakel, L. E. (2009, May). Clarification of assessment and evaluation. *Assessment Update, 21*(3), 8–9.

Langen, J. M. (2011). Evaluation of adjunct faculty in higher education institutions. *Assessment and Evaluation in Higher Education, 36*, 185–196.

Theall, M. (2010). Evaluating teaching: From reliability to accountability. *New Directions for Teaching and Learning, 123*, 85–95.

2

best practices in all forms of review and evaluation

Before we look at specific types of reviews, such as the annual evaluation or the promotion process, it's useful to consider a few practices that should occur in every type of review. In fact, I already referred to two of the most important practices in Chapter One:

- To understand what to review and how to review it requires understanding why you're conducting the review in the first place.
- Review processes should conclude whenever possible with a discussion of what's next and the setting of future goals.

In this chapter, we examine six other practices that can help make any type of review fairer to the person being evaluated and less stressful for you.

Practice 1: Follow your institution's established procedures to the letter

Problems arise in reviews more frequently because of a failure to follow established procedures than any other factor. U.S. courts have proven reluctant to intervene in the review processes of universities—except when an institution failed to follow its own policies (Poskanzer, 2002; Kaplin and Lee, 1995; Leap, 1993; Rebell, 1990; Copeland and Murry, 1996; Haskell, 1997). For this reason, regardless of the advice you receive from your colleagues and other written sources, including this book, be sure that everything you do is fully in accordance with all applicable procedures. A matter as seemingly insignificant as missing a notification date by a few days, following steps out of the prescribed order "because it seemed more logical to do so," or failing to use the form specified in the policy manual can disrupt an otherwise perfect process.

Perhaps the worst thing that can happen is for procedures at the department, division or college, and institutional levels to conflict with one another, making adherence to one set of guidelines a necessary violation of another set. If you suspect that this type of discrepancy might affect reviews in your area, administrators who are in a position to do so should take measures to resolve those differences before they begin to examine specific cases. Otherwise someone could claim that the procedures were modified only to help or harm the faculty member under review. If you find yourself in that situation, you'll have made the problem worse, not better. It's usually the case that policies established by higher administrative levels take precedence over those of lower administrative levels. In other words, colleges expect departments to align their policies with the college procedure, not vice versa. So you will need to make sure that you're familiar with all of your institution's applicable review policies, not merely those that you deal with most directly. In university systems, that means it's important to become aware of the requirements, deadlines, and general procedures of the central administration as well.

These are some of the common mistakes reviewers make when they don't follow their institution's established procedures:

○ Trying to be helpful in ways that ultimately prove to be unhelpful. We already saw in Chapter One that for legal reasons, certain institutions don't allow someone who has been denied tenure to learn the reasons for that decision. Out of a good-willed attempt to help the faculty member do better in his or her next position, some administrators offer guidance on how to improve and what to do differently next time. But this attempt to be helpful is tantamount to providing a reason for the denial. In the same way, in systems that require administrators to provide faculty members with reasons for negative decisions, it can be equally problematic to withhold information for fear of offering up grounds for a lawsuit. The old principle that no good deed goes unpunished is particularly true in the case of faculty reviews. The best course for reviewers to follow is to communicate with the applicant at precisely the level of detail the institutional policy requires—no more and no less.

   ◦ *Basing decisions on criteria other than those specified in institutional policy.* Most review procedures outline the criteria and standards that must be attained in order for a review to be successful, and some procedures even specify the weight that must be given to individual standards. Committees sometimes bring into their discussions knowledge and impressions that go far beyond these established criteria and standards. Someone might say, "I know these teaching evaluations look good, but when my son was in this professor's course, he *hated* it," or, "Her list of publications is impressive, but I suspect that her graduate students do most of the work." If the institution's guidelines call for instruction to be judged on the basis of teaching evaluations and research to be based on the number and quality of publications, then hearsay and suspicion have no place in the committee's decision. The sole exception to this rule is the matter of collegiality. U.S. courts have repeatedly ruled that it may be used as a criterion for review, even when not specified as a separate standard, since it, like showing up for work and telling the truth about your credentials, is essential to professional effectiveness in all three areas of teaching, research, and service (see *Mayberry v. Dees*, 1981; *University of Baltimore v. Iz*, 1998).

   ◦ *Waiving a criterion in a manner that unintentionally establishes a precedent.* Review processes occasionally struggle with how to handle a faculty member whose work has been exceptional except for one particular area: the superb teacher and campus leader who can't be tenured because of inadequate research; the world-renowned scholar who doesn't qualify for a merit increase because of tepid course evaluations; the wonderful advisor and mentor whose posttenure review is in jeopardy because his or her scholarly achievements have been lagging. There can be a great temptation in these cases to waive a criterion because of the person's extraordinary performance in other areas. "Isn't it more humane to bend the policy just a little," we may find ourselves asking, "because of the overall contribution this person is making?" Indeed, it seems so reasonable to retain or reward someone whose performance in certain areas strongly overshadows a deficiency elsewhere. But even if you don't intend to do so and your institution doesn't have a policy that allows you to waive a criterion, making that type of exception establishes a precedent that you and your successors will have to live with and defend for many years to come. Once a criterion is waived for one person, others, including those for whom you may want the policy rigidly enforced, will insist that what has been done for others should now be done for them. It's always bad practice to violate a policy in order to protect a specific individual. The far better strategy is to work with others to modify the policies so that special cases can be considered when exceptions are truly called for, while leaving the requirements intact for the majority of situations.

   ○ *Base all your conclusions on documented evidence, not mere impressions.* Just as it is vital for decisions to be made on the criteria that have actually been set, not on the criteria that the reviewer might prefer, all decisions in a review should be formed on the basis of clear, documented evidence, not on what the reviewer may believe or have heard about the faculty member. We are all tempted at times to allow our impressions of someone to affect our judgments of that person. We may think that someone can't possibly be a very good teacher because his or her remarks in conversation seem so trivial and dull, or we may not feel that another person's research has been effective because it is conducted in an area that we regard as insignificant. But if the person were to appeal a decision made on such a basis, it would be extremely difficult to justify our actions to others. It's not that the evidence we use has to be solely quantitative in nature. In Chapter Eleven, we'll encounter a number of highly effective ways in which documentation can be provided for achievements that don't easily lend themselves to quantification. Besides, merely counting publications or citing scores from student evaluations doesn't convey much information. Some publications may have been extremely brief and in journals that accept whatever submissions they receive. Some student ratings may have been based on a very small population of students, all of whom adore this particular professor, while the vast majority of those who enroll in his or her courses drop that section long before the surveys are conducted. The point is that the evidence used to make decisions has to be meaningful, objective, and clear to an impartial observer. A good test to determine whether your conclusion has been based on sufficient evidence is to ask yourself, "If this decision were to result in a lawsuit, would I have sufficient documentation to justify it to a skeptical observer in a court of law?"

Practice 2: Documented evidence should focus on observable behaviors and verifiable results, not on general impressions of the person's attitudes, opinions, or personality

The goal of a properly designed review process must always be to ensure a high standard of professional behavior and activity, always recognizing the freedom each person has to believe, feel, and desire whatever he or she wishes. Because of the nature of academic life, it can be particularly difficult to accomplish this goal when the opinion in question is one that the reviewer finds offensive, or the personality of the candidate displays characteristics dramatically different from the reviewer's own. Table 2.1 shows several specific examples of what most review systems would regard as acceptable in situations where a faculty member's behavior or attitude may be involved.

What makes the statements in the center column of Table 2.1 inappropriate is that the person making them has based his or her

Table 2.1 Personality Versus Behavior

Type / Issue	Unacceptable: Based on Attitude, Opinion, or Personality	Acceptable: Based on Behavior and Verifiable Activity
Racism	"Your worldview makes you nothing more than a bigot."	"Your refusal to work with advisees whose ethnicities differ from your own is clearly discriminatory and violates institutional policies."
Sexual orientation	"This department will not support the promotion of any faculty member who feels uncomfortable with the idea that Queer Studies is a legitimate academic discipline."	"By rejecting candidates for the position simply because they were homosexual, your practices have called the legitimacy of the entire search into question."
Use of profanity	"You apparently see nothing wrong with the use of vulgarities in everyday discourse."	"Your repeated and unnecessary use of profanity in the classroom is interfering with your pedagogical effectiveness because it is causing students either to drop your course or avoid attending your classes."
Conceit	"This last year has been a disaster because of your arrogance."	"Your dismissive remarks to your colleagues at faculty meetings are disruptive and often prevent the group from completing its full agenda."

Table 2.1 (*Continued*)

Type / Issue	Unacceptable: Based on Attitude, Opinion, or Personality	Acceptable: Based on Behavior and Verifiable Activity
Irritability	"This department already has more than its fair share of curmudgeons and can't afford to tenure another one."	"We've already lost two administrative assistants in the past three years who said that they wouldn't tolerate your abusive and petulant remarks. This behavior needs to change."
Reclusiveness	"You're simply too much of an introvert for us to appoint you to be chair of the committee."	"Your unwillingness to meet with the other members of the committee has severely hampered the group's ability to meet its goals."

judgments on a person's feelings, temperament, or convictions. There are two problems with conducting reviews in this way.

First, colleges and universities have no business whatsoever dictating a person's philosophy, political opinions, character traits, or emotions. (The sole exception occurs when a private institution is clearly devoted to the doctrines of a particular religious group as indicated by its mission statement, in which case it may require that employees support the beliefs and practices of that faith.) Institutions of higher education are intended to encourage independence of mind and thought, and they will be unable to achieve that goal if they don't live up to their own expectations in their personnel policies.

Second, the unacceptable statements in the table are not independently verifiable and thus can be readily challenged in an appeal or grievance. After all, what degree of irritability or conceit does the institution regard as excessive, and where is that policy written down? By contrast, the observations in the right-hand column are based on specific activities or behaviors that can be documented, substantiated by observation or evidence, and demonstrated to be contrary to the effective operation of the discipline.

As we explore these considerations, it's important to understand that the term *verifiable* when used in connection with faculty reviews is not intended to be a synonym for *measurable*. The management consultant Dick Grote (1996) has this recommendation:

> The key is *describing* good performance with words, not measuring it with numbers. In every case, a good job can be described in such a way that it can be verified. Measurability is not the goal; verifiability is. Not everything can be measured with numbers; some numbers are meaningless, and sometimes the most meaningful aspects of the work can only be described. Aim for verifiable performance standards. Numbers just happen to be easy to verify [p. 137].

This principle becomes particularly important when you're reviewing behaviors that are important for their effectiveness rather than their frequency. At the University of Notre Dame, for example, one of the guides to evaluating a faculty member's service contributions states, "In evaluating service, the quality and impact of a faculty member's contributions may be more important than the number of committees" (University of Notre Dame, 2010). We've all known faculty members whose résumés are filled with lists of committees, task forces, and community boards to which they were appointed but on which they made little contribution because they attended meetings infrequently. A clear, professionally focused statement of what the faculty member actually did in terms of service and why those actions were important matters far more than such metrics as the number of memberships held or the quantity of offices filled.

One area of faculty behavior in which objective and verifiable review is particularly important is the issue of collegiality. As we'll see in Chapter Eight, it's perfectly appropriate to use collegiality as a factor in personnel decisions even when an institution's policies and procedures don't identify it as a criterion for evaluation. But until there exists a recognized and widely accepted instrument that documents a faculty member's collegiality in a consistent manner, reviewers and administrators will have to develop their own means of authenticating breaches of collegiality in a fair and objective manner. The key to recognizing a legitimate breach of collegiality is to ask: *What specific harm to the program or institution resulted from the actions of the faculty member?* In other words, if the person's words or demeanor merely made others feel bad, uncomfortable, or annoyed, that situation alone is unlikely to make a compelling case that genuine harm was done. Colleges and universities exist to advance knowledge and understanding, not to make its employees feel comfortable. But if a program can demonstrate that students have left the major specifically because of a professor's abusive language, that his or her colleagues have applied for positions at other universities because of the professor's angry outbursts at faculty meetings, or that a donor has withdrawn a gift because of the professor's vicious and disrespectful remarks, that evidence may be used to support the contention that lack of collegiality has resulted in verifiable harm to the institution.

Practice 3: Use statistical measurements appropriately

Statistical methods have a definite role to play in review processes. They allow quantifiable data to be aggregated, thus making it easy for observers to spot overall patterns and trends. Nevertheless, statistical measurements are frequently misused in the review and evaluation of faculty members, partly because many administrators have no specific training in how the results of these tests are to be interpreted and partly because they give the illusion of objectivity even when the numbers generated by the formulae are absolutely meaningless. In this section, we examine the most common misuses of statistical measurements.

Overinterpretation of the results   Electronic spreadsheets allow the user to calculate numbers with a great deal of precision. But greater precision does not always mean greater accuracy. For instance, during faculty reviews, it is not unheard of to hear statements like the following: "The average score on this professor's teaching evaluations is only 3.40061, while the departmental average is 3.40121, so this person is basically below average. I don't think we ought to be recommending anyone who's below average." While electronic spreadsheets regularly calculate numbers to the fifteenth decimal place, that degree of precision has no real meaning for the type of data collected during faculty review processes. The general rule of thumb is to round your result to the lowest number of significant digits found in the data used to generate that result. Since a great deal of data analyzed from evaluation forms compels the reviewer to reply in whole numbers or on a Likert scale (which is then converted to whole numbers), averages should also be reported as whole numbers. At the very most, it may be useful to examine averages of these scores rounded to a single decimal point. Any conclusions drawn from results calculated to the hundredths place or smaller is almost certainly of no statistical merit whatsoever.

Misunderstanding of averages   One of the reasons that results are often calculated to the hundredths or thousandths of a point is that review procedures regularly calculate averages as means (the sum of all scores divided by the number of scores). Means are appropriate methods of calculating averages when a respondent is allowed to enter any value along a sliding scale. Thus, if a form allows someone to respond with a number like 2.675 or 3.41 when asked to provide a score between 1 and 5, calculation of means may well be informative. (It would be fair to ask on what basis the reviewer developed such a precise rating as 2.675.) But most evaluation forms require the respondent to fill in a bubble or circle a whole number on a scale; if a respondent circles two adjacent numbers on the scale, most systems will calculate the result as ending in .5 to indicate that the answer was somewhere between those two numbers.

What this means is that the system used for the review requires the user to answer with discrete data rather than continuous data, and means are not the appropriate way to average numbers when examining discrete data. In those cases, calculation of the median provides a more meaningful result. Spreadsheets can of course calculate medians just as readily as they can calculate means, and for a small number of responses, this type of average is even easier to calculate by hand: simply arrange all responses in order from lowest to highest and select the middle value (if the number of responses is odd) or the mean of the middle two values (if the number of responses is even). Use of the median when analyzing discrete data avoids both the problem of overinterpretation and the impact that a few outliers can have on the results. Imagine, for example, a department of fourteen people where the vast majority of the members believe that the chair is doing a superb job, while three disgruntled faculty members wish to punish their supervisor for their own unhappiness. If nine people give the chair a 5 on the question of, "To what degree is this administrator effective?" and the three provide a score of 1, the mean for this item will be 4.142857143, while the median will be 5. The effect of the outliers is thus eliminated.

Using only averages to analyze data   Averages are one useful way of identifying patterns in data when they are calculated properly. But they are not the only useful statistical measurement that reviewers can adopt. Standard deviations can help determine the degree to which the respondents to a survey question agreed with one another in their replies. For instance, in our hypothetical department of fourteen faculty members, suppose that another question about the chair was, "To what degree does this administrator maintain posted office hours?" In this case, even the three disgruntled faculty members may feel compelled to assign the chair a score of 5. Both questions result in a median of 5. But the question about effectiveness generates a standard deviation of 1.7, while the question about maintaining office hours generates a standard deviation of 0. In general, the higher the standard deviation, the greater the degree of disagreement in the data. By considering standard deviations, therefore, the reviewer might be prompted to examine the raw data more closely for certain questions, thus discovering that there are three faculty members whose replies differ radically from the responses of the other eleven.

Assumption that all items in a review possess equal merit   The example of a department chair evaluation that we've been considering also points to another issue commonly encountered in review processes: not all survey items are created equal. Many people, for example, might consider a chair's overall effectiveness to be a far more important issue than his or her maintenance of posted office hours. After all, a chair who is regularly three to five minutes late in the morning because of the need to drop off his or her children at the day-care center might be scored low in "timeliness" (if the department happens to be particularly persnickety—a condition not entirely unknown in certain universities), but extremely high in effectiveness. If the institution has a practice of calculating an overall score simply by averaging every item on the review form, less significant items will have the same weight as highly significant items, producing a result that is not as informative as it could be. It is far better to calculate overall scores only from a certain number of survey items generally agreed to be the most important questions on the form than to treat every question equally.

An alternative approach is to assign items a significance score so that very important items receive five to ten times the amount of impact in the total result. (To calculate a weighted average, simply multiply both the sum of the scores and the number of scores by the same weighted value before adding them to the other scores to be used in determining the overall average.) The Arreola model, which we'll consider in Chapter Ten, is particularly effective at emphasizing the most important factors while giving less significant issues less weight.

The worst possible practice that institutions can follow is to try to calculate overall averages by averaging the averages themselves. The problem with this method can be seen if we consider the case of a faculty member who is teaching one section of 120 students, another section of 50 students, and a third section of 4 students. Let's imagine that the largest class believes the faculty member is terrific, the midsize class thinks that the professor is very good, but the small class (a remedial section of an advanced course that the students are required to take because they were unsuccessful in an earlier class) resents the instructor and reflects their unhappiness on the course evaluation. Let's further imagine that on the item, "Rate the overall teaching effectiveness of this professor from 1 (very poor) to 5 (excellent)," the large class produces a median of 5 (mean 4.7, standard deviation .46), the midsized class a median of 4 (mean 4.1, standard deviation .46), and the small class a median of 1 (mean 1.3, standard deviation .5). If the institution produces what it regards as an overall average simply by averaging these averages—3.4 for both means and medians—the resulting number tells you nothing at all. The institution has weighted the class of 4 exactly equal to the class of 120. If we treat each student, not each class, as of equal weight, the results end up being quite different: the median is 5, the mean is 4, and the standard deviation is .71. The overall story is thus much clearer: this professor is widely regarded as an effective teacher by the vast majority of his or her students, while a small number of students strongly disagree for some (as yet unknown) reason. The results might prompt the reviewer to determine whether the students who scored the professor low have anything in common, and once this analysis is made, the reviewer's interpretation of the data will probably be much more accurate.

Practice 4: Make actual judgments when conducting summative evaluations; don't merely summarize data

One of the greatest challenges for administrators and faculty members who are new to the review process is drawing a firm conclusion from the information they consider. There's a strong tendency for reviewers simply to repeat the data provided in the application—"You published two articles in first-tier journals and three in second-tier journals over the last six years"—without ever making a judgment as to whether that level of performance is good or bad. The reviewer never says, "This rate of publication fails to meet the standards expected in our discipline, and thus I am unable to recommend you for promotion at this time," and the faculty member may assume that his or her productivity was satisfactory.

Failure to make clear judgments is particularly problematic in annual evaluations, which we'll consider in Chapter Four. By simply summarizing the information contained in a faculty member's annual report, you may send a misleading message to the person being reviewed and create a problem for yourself if a later negative decision is appealed. One of the most common questions asked when a challenge is made to a negative decision in a major evaluation is, "Was there a clear paper trail of warnings leading up to this conclusion?" If examination of the annual evaluations demonstrates that the faculty member had not been given a clear indication that adequate progress was not being made, it's possible that your decision will be overturned and your administrative status may even be placed in jeopardy. While your institutional policies will probably dictate which method of making judgments you must use, Dick Grote (1996) identifies four preferred ways of making sure that you're genuinely evaluative when conducting reviews:

1. Numerical rating scales, such as 1 to 5 or 1 to 10, where one end of the scale clearly indicates superior performance and the other end of the scale clearly indicates inadequate performance
2. Verbal rating scales based on the frequency of a desired behavior, ranging from Always to Never, as long as it is apparent that the low ends of this scale indicates inadequate performance
3. Rating scales based on what Grote calls an evaluation concept, but which we might regard as a level of quality, such as A to F, Outstanding to Unsatisfactory, or five stars to no stars
4. Verbal rating scales based on an expected standard of performance, such as "greatly exceeds the standard" through "does not meet the standard" or "exceeds expectations" through "does not meet expectations"

Practice 5: Remember that you already know more than you think you do

All of this discussion about following institutional policies to the letter and using statistics properly may make it appear that conducting faculty reviews is a highly complex task that you couldn't possibly master. Nothing could be further from the truth.

You already know far more about conducting effective reviews and evaluations than you think you do. Consider, for example, how you'd want the process to proceed if you (or perhaps one of your children) were undergoing a formal evaluation. You'd want the person who was conducting the review to be fair, constructive, and honest. You'd hate to think that the outcome of the process had already been determined before you had a reasonable opportunity to present your case. You'd want your imperfections seen in light of a larger context; perhaps these are areas in which you could now work for improvement, or perhaps the situation was a little more complex than it might initially appear. You'd want to receive adequate credit for your accomplishments and specific, helpful advice on how to do an even better job in the future. You'd want to know that the reviewer had your best interests in mind, as well as the best interests of the program and institution. And you'd want to know that people have read carefully—and given due consideration to—the supporting documentation you had so painstakingly assembled.

The truth is that everyone wants his or her review handled in this way. You are thus likely to produce far more useful evaluations, experience fewer appeals and grievances, and help your faculty members to a much greater extent if you frequently check yourself throughout the review process by asking this question: am I acting in a way that I would want the reviewer to act if I were the faculty member being evaluated at this time?

Practice 6: Don't overlook the value of 360-degree review processes

Finally it's important to take into account the insights that can be seen from more than your perspective alone. The 360-degree review takes full advantage of what can be learned from the people someone supervises, as well as that person's peers and supervisor. The goal is thus to ascertain how someone interacts with all kinds of stakeholders and to learn what he or she is like to work with and for, not merely what the supervisor alone may see. Nevertheless, in order for this type of review to be conducted properly, there are several important principles to keep in mind. To begin, remember what each observer is in the best position to notice and what he or she is largely unsuited or unqualified to evaluate. Too many 360-degree review processes ask the same questions of subordinates, peers, and supervisors even though their interactions are of very different kinds. For example, in the evaluation of a faculty member, students are well positioned to comment about whether graded materials were returned in a timely manner, the degree to which they felt appropriately challenged by a professor, whether the professor canceled or cut short classes frequently, the degree to which the professor addressed multiple learning styles, whether the professor tended to honor his or her posted office hours, and the professor's effectiveness in communication.

Students are not in a proper position to evaluate the professor's level of knowledge about his or her discipline, the appropriateness of the professor's pedagogical methods to the subject being taught, whether the professor's grading scale was too hard or too easy, or the degree to which the professor was a professional and collegial member of the department. The latter questions are matters that the person's peers in the discipline are in the best position to review, although they themselves may not have a broad enough perspective to answer questions typically addressed to administrators such as a professor's rate of progress toward tenure, adherence to institutional policies, or effectiveness in service to the discipline, college, or university.

Carefully designed and targeted questions for each constituency in a 360-degree evaluation will produce much more meaningful results for both the institution and the faculty member under review. (For more on the theory and practice of 360-degree approaches, see Ivancevich, Konopaske, and Matteson, 2010, and Edwards and Ewen, 1996. For an example of a well-designed form for rating the teaching effectiveness of a faculty colleague, see Braskamp and Ory, 1994.)

o conclusion

This chapter's reference to 360-degree evaluation may lead many readers to raise the question often asked about any type of faculty review: Are there actual insights to be gained from student course evaluations, or do students simply give higher scores to professors who are easier graders, more popular, and less demanding? Fortunately, this topic has generated a vast number of studies, and the results clearly and conclusively demonstrate that you can find a great deal of support for practically any position on this matter you prefer. For instance, you can find research suggesting that there is little correlation between student evaluation scores and the amount of learning that occurs in the course (Clayson, 2009). Other research finds that student evaluations are:

- Relatively valid as an indicator of effective teaching and relatively unaffected by bias (Marsh, 1984)
- Largely independent of superficial factors such as instructor popularity, rank, and tendency to give high grades (Aleamoni, 1999)
- Significantly affected by an instructor's tendency to give high grades and inversely related to class size (Hamilton, 1980)
- Closely correlated with such factors as the instructor's extraversion and agreeableness (Patrick, 2011)
- Highly correlated with the student's academic level, such as freshman versus senior, undergraduate versus graduate, and the like (Aleamoni and Graham, 1974)
- Unrelated to the students' level of commitment to the subject and course (Beran and Violato, 2009)
- Inversely related to class size (Crittenden, Norr, and LeBailly, 1975)
- Inversely related (although only weakly) to class size (Feldman, 1984)
- Reflective of students' perceptions about the difficulty of the course (Addison, Best, and Warrington, 2006)
- Probably more statistically reliable and valid than any other form of evaluating instruction (Cashin, 1995)

- Of no more utility than product popularity surveys (Lewis, 2006)
- Of highly variable utility overall (Beran, Violato, Kline, and Frideres, 2005)

It's only a slight exaggeration to say that if you search hard enough, you can find studies confirming any hypothesis you like about factors that affect scores on student ratings of instruction, as well as studies disproving that very same hypothesis. Braskamp and Ory (1994) provide an excellent overview of some of the most important studies done in this area. Best practices would suggest, therefore, that in systems where student course evaluations are a required component of faculty reviews, the reviewer should:

- Focus solely on factors that students are in the best position to judge
- Look for consistent patterns rather than limited sets of data; for example, don't place too much emphasis on comments made by an extremely small number of students or disparities found in one particular course
- Analyze student evaluation data according to the statistical methods appropriate for the types of information collected, as discussed in this chapter
- Not use student ratings as the sole method of determining teaching effectiveness but combine them with other approaches, such as peer and supervisor observations, student success rates in subsequent courses, review of course syllabi or teaching portfolios, and indicators of teaching excellence like the attainment of awards and certifications
- Examine student ratings of the instructor within multiple contexts, such as comparable courses and class sizes in the department, similar courses at peer institutions, and the instructor's own progress over time

References

Addison, W. E., Best, J., & Warrington, J. D. (2006). Students' perceptions of course difficulty and their ratings of the instructor. *College Student Journal, 40*, 409–416.

Aleamoni, L. M. (1999). Student rating myths versus research facts from 1924 to 1998. *Journal of Personnel Evaluation in Education, 13,* 153–66.

Aleamoni, L. M., & Graham, M. H. (1974). The relationship between CEQ ratings and instructor's rank, class size and course level. *Journal of Educational Measurement, 11,* 189–202.

Beran, T., & Violato, C. (2009). Student ratings of teaching effectiveness: Student engagement and course characteristics. *Canadian Journal of Higher Education, 39*(1), 1–13.

Beran, T., Violato, C., Kline, D., & Frideres, J. (2005). The utility of student ratings of instruction for students, faculty, and administrators: A "consequential validity" study. *Canadian Journal of Higher Education, 2,* 49–70.

Braskamp, L. A., & Ory, J. C. (1994). *Assessing faculty work: Enhancing individual and institutional performance.* San Francisco: Jossey-Bass.

Cashin, W. E. (1995, September). *Student ratings of teaching: The research revisited.* IDEA Paper No. 32. Retrieved June 3, 2011, from http://www.theideacenter.org/sites/default/files/Idea_Paper_32.pdf.

Clayson, D. E. (2009). Student evaluations of teaching: Are they related to what students learn? A meta-analysis and review of the literature. *Journal of Marketing Education, 31*(1), 16–30.

Copeland, J. D., & Murry, J. W., Jr. (1996). Getting tossed from the ivory tower. *Missouri Law Review, 61,* 233–327.

Crittenden, K. S., Norr, J. L., & LeBailly, R. K. (1975). Size of university classes and student evaluation of teaching. *Journal of Higher Education, 46,* 461–470.

Edwards, M. R., & Ewen, A. J. (1996). *360 feedback: The powerful new model for employee assessment and performance improvement.* New York: AMACOM.

Feldman, K. A. (1984). Class size and college students' evaluations of teachers and courses: A closer look. *Research in Higher Education, 21*(1), 45–116.

Grote, R. C. (1996). *The complete guide to performance appraisal.* New York: AMACOM.

Hamilton, L. C. (1980). Grades, class size, and faculty status predict teaching evaluations. *Teaching Sociology, 8*(1), 47–62.

Haskell, R. E. (1997, August). Academic freedom, promotion, reappointment, tenure and the administrative use of student evaluation of faculty (SEF): (Part III) Analysis and implications of views from the court in relation to accuracy and psychometric validity. *Education Policy Analysis Archives,* Vol. 5(18). Retrieved from epaa.asu.edu/epaa/v5n18.html#marker_section5a.

Ivancevich, J. M., Konopaske, R., & Matteson, M. T. (2010). *Organizational behavior and management* (9th ed.). New York: McGraw-Hill.

Kaplin, W. A., & Lee, B. A. (1995). *The law of higher education: A comprehensive guide to legal implications of administrative decision making.* San Francisco: Jossey-Bass.

Leap, T. L. (1993). *Tenure, discrimination, and the courts.* Ithaca, NY: ILR Press.

Lewis, H. R. (2006). *Excellence without a soul: How a great university forgot education.* New York: Public Affairs.

Marsh, H. W. (1984). Students' evaluations of university teaching: Dimensionality, reliability, validity, potential biases, and utility. *Journal of Educational Psychology, 76,* 707–54.

Mayberry v. Dees. (1981). 663 F.2d 502 (4th Cir. Ct.).

Patrick, C. L. (2011). Student evaluations of teaching: Effects of the Big Five personality traits, grades and the validity hypothesis. *Assessment and Evaluation in Higher Education, 36,* 239–249

Poskanzer, S. G. (2002). *Higher education law: The faculty.* Baltimore, MD: Johns Hopkins University Press.

Rebell, M. A. (1990). Legal issues concerning teacher evaluation. In J. Millman & L. Darling-Hammond (Eds.). *The new handbook of teacher evaluation* (pp. 337–355). Thousand Oaks, CA: Sage.

University of Baltimore v. Iz.(1998). 716 A.2d 1107 (Md. Ct. App.).

University of Notre Dame. (2010). *Best practices: Service; Women in Arts and Letters.* Retrieved from http://wal.nd.edu/commitment-to-women/best-practices-service/.

3

oral and written reviews and evaluations

In this chapter as in many of those that follow, we'll explore a number of mini-case studies that are designed to allow you to practice your own evaluative techniques in a safe and constructive setting. The goal isn't to get the answer right—in many cases, the answer will depend on your institution's policies and your own individual style—but rather to help you think through a challenging situation before you next encounter the problems that can arise when reviewing a faculty member. We get better at evaluation, like so many other activities, the more we do it, and these mini-case studies are intended to give you practice in situations that are relevant to the chapter where they appear.

The results of a review are sometimes conveyed to faculty members solely orally or solely in writing, but it's common to combine these two approaches for bringing the review to a close. Not every system conducts those two parts in the same order. It may be that the faculty member receives a formal, written notification of the result, followed by a meeting where questions can be asked and issues explored in some depth. It may be that an administrator conveys the result orally to the faculty member first, with a memo of understanding prepared later. Or it may be that the written notification is handed to the faculty member in a meeting, with the oral and written notifications occurring almost simultaneously.

In any case, it's important for anyone who will be conducting faculty reviews and evaluations to be aware of the best practices, limitations, and special features of both oral and written processes in order to conduct reviews most effectively. Although there are many advantages to conducting formative evaluations orally, summative evaluations in writing, and formative-summative evaluations with a blend of oral and written, most institutional processes don't offer that choice. For this reason, we'll also explore some cautions to keep in mind if your institution requires you to conduct certain types of reviews in certain ways.

○ oral reviews

An oral review is any conference between a supervisor and a faculty member in which the faculty member's performance is examined and recommendations are made. More formal than a spontaneous mentoring session, oral reviews usually involve a discussion of assigned duties, accomplishments during the review period, and the establishment of new goals for the future.

Advantages and Limitations

While colleges and universities need a paper trail of the evaluation process for a variety of reasons (including accreditation requirements, legal protection and, in many cases, the policies of their governing boards), oral reviews have certain advantages that aren't possible in a written evaluation. For one thing, they allow the faculty member to ask immediate questions about issues that seem unclear and to address conclusions with which he or she disagrees. Second, they allow the reviewer to go into far greater detail than is usually possible in a written evaluation, particularly when institutions impose rigid formats for these documents. Third, they make goal setting, which we'll explore in greater depth in Chapter 4, far easier to conduct; the give-and-take that must occur in order to achieve a mutually acceptable list of goals will be awkward and time-consuming if it has to take place through exchange of written documents. Finally, they can be far freer in form than is usually possible in a written evaluation.

If the faculty member immediately understands and accepts one topic of the discussion, the reviewer can spend more time on matters for which there's less agreement or pursue additional topics that the faculty member wishes to address. Oral reviews are in many ways the best possible format for formative evaluations since the reviewer can ask the faculty member to reflect on a weakness or challenge and listen to the reply, and the two of them can jointly explore ways for the faculty member to do better in the future. But even in summative evaluations, oral summaries have value. They allow the reviewer to share in the faculty member's joy at a positive result, present negative results in a manner that can be much more humane than compelling the recipient to see cold words on the page, and explain results that may not immediately seem distinctly positive or negative. The prime example of the last situation is a denial of tenure that can be reversed if certain conditions are met. The reviewer can describe the reasons for what may appear to be a mixed message and elucidate what needs to be done from this point forward.

Nevertheless, oral evaluations are not suitable or appropriate for every situation. The reviewer and the faculty member may have significantly different recollections of what was said and agreed on during the evaluation, and disagreements over these issues could arise later. Even in a formative evaluation, the reviewer will have no indisputable record of what he or she advised the faculty member to do in the case of a misunderstanding or lack of follow-through. Faculty members may be nervous, angry, or preoccupied during an oral evaluation, making them far more likely to forget key points than they would if they could reread a written summary as often as they liked. Oral reviews can also be very time-consuming; with written evaluations, reviewers tend to include a great deal of boilerplate, with the result that it can take a lot less time to write a review than to meet about one. For those who supervise a large number of faculty members, there may not be enough flexibility in the schedule to conduct more than a brief meeting with every person.

Finally, reviewers vary widely in their interpersonal skills, and the person who may be the most effective at identifying a faculty member's strengths and weaknesses may be the least effective at verbalizing those issues face-to-face in a potentially stressful meeting. In fact, one study found that at least among managers in the corporate world, face-to-face performance appraisals were usually the most anxiety-producing duty they had (O'Brien, 2000). Most administrators in higher education probably feel the same. So although there are great benefits to be gained from including an oral review in most evaluation processes, there's also need for caution so that what is said (and can't be taken back) doesn't create difficulties later.

Best Practices for Oral Evaluations

In *Organizational Behavior and Management* (2010), John Ivancevich, Robert Konopaske, and Michael Matteson outline four best practices that studies have demonstrated to be useful whenever evaluations contain an oral component:

> Research and the practical implementation of feedback provide ways feedback can improve performance. First, give feedback frequently, not once a year at a performance evaluation session. Second, permit the evaluated person to participate in feedback sessions. This serves as a two-way exchange, problem-solving approach rather than an "evaluator telling" method. When employees participate they are usually more satisfied with the feedback communication. Third, in providing feedback, do not solely focus on ineffective performance or problems. Praise, recognition, and encouragement serve as a form of positive reinforcement. Fourth, address results, goals, and goals accomplished, and not performer characteristics. A golden rule of gaining and maintaining the respect of subordinates (evaluated

employees) is to not attack or discuss their personality, attitudes, or values. These four guidelines are not perfect, nor do they always work effectively, but they are supported by research and they are not difficult to implement [pp. 184–185. The research referred to in the passage is Herold, Parsons, and Rensvold, 1996, and Van Fleet, Peterson, and Van Fleet, 2005.]

To these four practices—frequency of review, encouraging two-way conversations, mixing positive reinforcement with discussion of weaknesses, and focusing on behaviors, not personalities—we can add several others that are likely to increase the effectiveness of oral evaluations.

Conduct the oral evaluation in its own meeting, and state the result of the evaluation at the beginning

In order to emphasize the importance of oral evaluations, they should be given their own meetings, not combined with discussion of other issues. Conducting an evaluation as part of some other conversation trivializes the review or may cause the faculty member to lose sight of important issues due to all the other topics also covered. Scheduling an evaluation session as a separate meeting allows both you and the person who's being reviewed to prepare questions that need to be asked and to get into the proper frame of mind for what should be regarded as a very serious activity.

To reinforce this idea, start the formal evaluation with a summary of what your conclusion is going to be. (Suggested phrasing for statements of this kind, designed for a range of reviews from the very positive to the strongly negative, can be found in Buller, 2006.) The faculty member is going to be eager to know how well he or she did, and if you don't define the direction you're going in at the beginning of the meeting, you may discover that important points don't receive the person's full attention. So regardless of whether the news is good or bad, don't keep the faculty member hanging. State the result, and then use the rest of the meeting to demonstrate how you arrived at it.

State any goals that you develop in a form that is as clear and specific as possible, and establish a measurable standard to indicate whether that goal has been achieved

Vague goals are not at all helpful to the faculty member you're reviewing. Telling people to "teach better" or "become more active in research" doesn't provide the type of guidance they need in order to meet your expectations. But in oral evaluations, not providing clear enough guidance is also unhelpful for you. At some point in the future, you'll need to indicate to the faculty member whether the goals you've set have been achieved. Unless you've expressed those goals in a manner that allows an objective observer to know for sure that the standard has or has not been met, you're merely creating a future problem for yourself.

As difficult as it can be in such disciplines as the arts and humanities where faculty members sometimes believe that we overquantify information in higher education and thus distort the complexity of the human experience, standards expressed in numerical form are the easiest for most people to understand

As an example, everyone who works in a given discipline has at least a general understanding of what is meant by such statements as "three additional peer-reviewed articles accepted for publication" or "raising the median score on student course evaluations by at least half a point." If you find it absolutely impossible to quantify the goal you have in mind, at least come to a clear agreement about what you're requiring. Discuss with the faculty member whether "increased grant activity" means a larger number of proposals submitted, a larger number of proposals funded, larger amounts sought by the proposals, or simply the identification of additional sources for external funding. Make it clear how you will recognize that the person's teaching has become "more active in nature" or that the students are making "better progress." If you don't define these terms carefully now, it'll be all but impossible to do so when you're deciding whether the goal has been achieved.

Reiterate at the end of the meeting the overall result of the evaluation with which you began

If an oral evaluation is properly done, the discussion that occurs should be comprehensive and of some length. You will have reviewed the faculty member's achievements in each relevant area, provided some examples, set goals for the future, responded to a number of questions, and provided whatever additional advice seems most appropriate. That's a lot of territory to cover, and you don't want the main thrust of the meeting to become lost. A highly positive evaluation can begin to feel like a rejection when, after an encouraging opening, a long list of improvements is suggested. Similarly, a warning that inadequate progress is being made can quickly be overshadowed by consoling reminders that the situation is far from hopeless and that the faculty has many important achievements to his or her credit. For this reason, oral evaluations should both begin and end with an emphasis on the primary message you want the faculty member to take away. Unlike written evaluations, an oral review isn't something that the faculty member can go over again later. You need to make your central point memorable, and the best way to do that is to begin and end on this same theme.

Follow up the meeting with a memorandum of understanding

As a further way of making sure that the message you sent is exactly the same as what the faculty member received, send a memo containing your major points after the meeting. Keep a copy of the memo in your file so that you'll have a record of what you said and the recommendations that you made. Even better, send the faculty member two copies of the memo, with instructions to sign and return one of them, indicating that he or she has received and read the document. In that way, you'll have a way of verifying the substance of the meeting if there is ever a claim that certain matters were not addressed or that the requirements you imposed were different from what the faculty member now says they were.

mini-case studies: conducting oral evaluations

In accordance with your institution's procedures, you're conducting a series of oral evaluations for faculty members who work in your area. For some reason, this year's set of evaluations seems more plagued with problems than usual. What do you do in each case, and is there anything you could have done to prevent each problem from occurring?

o   o   o

You had expected the first evaluation to go smoothly because everything you had to report was positive. The faculty member is excellent in teaching, has recently received significant grants that have resulted in important publications, and is regularly the most valuable member on committees. But after you congratulate the faculty member for all these accomplishments, you're surprised by the reaction: "Then why didn't I get a larger raise this year? I know I'm getting a bigger increase than anyone else in my department, but it's still not enough. If I've done as well as you said, I'm offended that you're not following all those compliments with news of a significant salary adjustment."

o   o   o

The second evaluation requires you to review with the faculty member a combination of strengths and weaknesses. You cite all of the person's accomplishments, provide what you believe to be constructive advice on how to do even better, and conclude by outlining the progress that'll be required in order for the faculty member's upcoming promotion hearing to be successful. The meeting ends on what appears to be a friendly note, and so you're shocked to learn later that the faculty member claims you made wholly inappropriate remarks during the oral evaluation. In a complaint submitted to your superior, you are described as having made suggestive remarks that, when the faculty member objected, became abusive and intimidating.

o o o

You expected the third review to be challenging, but it turned out to be even more confrontational than you had anticipated. The faculty member has been performing poorly in nearly all areas. Students who take the professor's courses routinely give low evaluations and do worse in their subsequent courses than students who had studied with others in that discipline. This professor's research activity is sparse and consists of only an online book review and a short essay unrelated to the faculty member's discipline. The faculty member is regularly appointed or elected to committees but has a record of missing meetings or failing to complete assigned duties. You go through these concerns, being as constructive as you can, only to be called a racist because you and the faculty member are of different ethnicities. "You never liked me from the moment I started working here and," charges the faculty member, "with the assignments you've given me, I've never had a real chance to excel at my teaching and research. Everything you've talked about today isn't my problem; it's your problem."

o written evaluations

Written evaluations are often conducted in addition to or instead of an oral review session. The memo of understanding resulting from an oral review that we considered earlier is a form of written evaluation, although many institutions also have their own forms or templates.

Advantages and Limitations

Many colleges and universities prefer written evaluations to oral review sessions because they provide documentation that can be used to justify promotions and merit increases or to provide evidence when faculty members must be reprimanded or dismissed. Written evaluations usually can—and probably should—be reviewed by the author's supervisor, the office of human resources, or university counsel before they are presented to the faculty member so as to make sure that they adhere to institutional policy and don't contain any language that could prove to be problematic.

Documents allow for multiple revisions and permit a degree of advance planning that is not always possible in an oral evaluation. Sitting face-to-face with a faculty member and responding to follow-up questions, the reviewer can easily say things that he or she had not intended to bring up or use language that may be misinterpreted. By writing out an evaluation, the reviewer has time to reflect on each statement and amend any phrasing that on rereading appears to be undesirable. Furthermore, the evaluation doesn't have to be conducted in a single sitting. At the beginning of a review period, the supervisor can prepare a blank word processing document for each person who will need to be evaluated. Then as achievements occur or challenges arise, the reviewer can make a note of these in the document to incorporate when the evaluation is polished later. That practice allows the reviewer to cite specific examples of instances in which the faculty member's performance could have been improved. It is also far less likely that a significant accomplishment is going to be overlooked when a number of evaluations must be prepared in a short amount of time. Finally, many institutions require a standard format or scoring system for written evaluations, making the information conveyed to faculty members far more consistent than may be possible during an oral review.

Nevertheless, despite all these advantages, written evaluations are also limiting in a number of ways. They don't allow the give-and-take of an oral review, and faculty members can't stop you to ask about issues that they find unclear or inaccurate. Once an evaluation is committed to writing, it becomes almost permanent—even if the information in it is wrong or you believe that all the copies have been destroyed. (People frequently keep photocopies of documents they believe will be useful to them later, particularly when there has been conflict between them and their supervisor.) When the format of a written evaluation is specified by an institution, reviewers may not be able to address all the points they believe are relevant for each individual. Moreover, it's almost impossible to write a review that's long enough to address all the facets of any individual faculty member's performance. For this reason, oral reviews can be much more comprehensive than most written evaluations and offer the faculty member a more nuanced interpretation of the strengths and weaknesses that are relevant to his or her position. Written evaluations are thus extremely important methods of documenting the result of a review process, but they are far from a perfect mechanism for improving faculty performance unless they're also accompanied by individual consultations, mentoring, development opportunities, and formal procedures that allow the person to respond to the evaluation.

Best Practices for Written Evaluations

At the University of Tennessee, Knoxville, the Office of the Provost and Senior Vice Chancellor for Academic Affairs has developed a comprehensive manual for faculty evaluation that concludes with a series of best practice statements for all types of faculty review and evaluation (http://provost.utk.edu/docs/evaluation/faculty-evaluation-manual. pdf). Among the recommendations offered with regard to written evaluations are these:

- Written evaluation of teaching should include 360-degree analysis since a faculty member's students, peers, and supervisors each have their own perspectives and unique areas of expertise or opportunities for observation.
- Written evaluations should provide an opportunity for a faculty member to conduct a self-evaluation since the individual's own

frame of reference can help to place accomplishments or challenges into their proper contexts.

- Written evaluations should indicate clearly whether the faculty member exceeds, meets, or fails to meet a specified standard that is articulated in a formal written document, such as a department's bylaws. If evaluations are conducted without reference to established standards and rubrics, faculty members may end up being uncertain whether they are still failing to meet their supervisor's objectives rather than making desirable and incremental improvements.

- While student evaluations are important, they should not be given greater weight than other factors in personnel decisions simply because they are easily quantifiable.

- The department chair's evaluation of a faculty member's teaching should focus on three key areas: the appropriateness of course content to programmatic goals; the effectiveness of the grading system, standards, and evaluation tools to promote the desired level of student performance; and the suitability of the teaching methods to the discipline.

- Evaluation of research, scholarship, and creative activities should include review not only of "output activities" (such as publications, presentations, and grants received), but also "input activities" (such as adhering to high ethical standards in all scholarly activities, expending sufficient time and energy in research activities, and taking personal responsibility for one's own scholarly and creative growth).

- Evaluation of service should emphasize activities that are highly relevant to the faculty member's professional position and not those that, although commendable, fall largely outside the scope of the institution's mission.

- Evaluations of service should address contributions to the institution (including the faculty member's department and college or division), discipline, and profession as a scholar. In other words, committees are not the only way in which a faculty member's service can enhance the institution's mission. Constructive contributions to one's discipline as a whole can help bring the college or university international recognition. Improving the public's perception of what college professors do can enhance recruitment efforts, the search for external funding, and support for education as a national priority.

While these observations and others contained in the manual developed by the University of Tennessee, Knoxville, are an excellent summary of best practices in written evaluation, a number of other recommendations might also be made. These additions are particularly helpful for reviewers who are less experienced in or nervous about the practice of putting their judgments about faculty members into a written form.

To begin, since written evaluations become a permanent record, always leave sufficient time between when you complete them and when you present them to the faculty members being reviewed. Sufficient time means at least one full day, although two full weeks are far better. Sentences that appear clear and indisputable to you today may well seem ambiguous or ill advised when you read them a week or two from now. The pressure of getting multiple evaluations done within a limited time sometimes causes reviewers to complete their work only shortly before the reports are due to the faculty members. By not allowing yourself sufficient time to reconsider, rephrase, and revise written evaluations, you could cause problems for yourself and your institution that could easily have been avoided. A basic rule of thumb should be never to send out a written evaluation that hasn't been allowed to mature for at least twenty-four hours.

Second, as Dick Grote (1996) suggests, "Keep it simple" (p. 333). Address the points that need to be addressed, either because they are required by your institution's procedures or because they have had a significant effect on the faculty member's performance of his or her assigned duties, and let other matters go. Those secondary points can always be broached in a mentoring session, oral follow-up to the written review, or an informal conversation. Putting extraneous observations into a written evaluation merely increases the likelihood that the faculty member will raise objections later.

Third, reread the evaluation from the perspective of the recipient. Words that can seem friendly in person often appear cold and abrupt on the page. Irony does not come through in a written evaluation. (Try saying, "Well, that's the most brilliant idea I've ever heard!" once as though you meant it and once as though you were being ironic. In person, nuances of inflection are often obvious, but they are all but impossible to detect in a document.) Examine the letter or form for any remark that even unintentionally may come across as dismissive, condescending, or insensitive by someone who differs from you in gender, ethnicity, sexual orientation, age, marital status, or level of disability.

Fourth, within the allowable limits of confidentiality, have someone else look over the evaluation before you send it, particularly if the review is in any way negative. Most systems allow you to run the evaluation by your own supervisor for his or her consideration. It's almost always possible, and often highly desirable, to have legal counsel or the office of human resources review a draft of your evaluation. Other people may spot potential problems in the document that you can't discern because you've been so directly involved in developing the text. Their advice is at least worth considering.

Finally, consider your evaluation in the context of the faculty member's other evaluations if you have access to them. Reviewers often regard each evaluation as an isolated process. In certain ways, that view is appropriate, but in other ways, it can lead to difficulties. For example, if you're producing an annual evaluation, how does this review fit into the trajectory of those that came before it? If the review demonstrates consistency or an ongoing trend of either improvement or decline, the pattern should be easy to defend. But if it represents a sudden shift in direction—such as a glowing evaluation after years of harsh criticism or a lukewarm evaluation after many years of praise—be prepared to justify precisely what you believe to have changed this year and why your evaluation seems so different from earlier ones. In a similar way, a negative tenure decision after consistently positive annual evaluations will need to be thoroughly justified if (or more likely when) it's challenged. Remember that even if you regard the evaluation as a snapshot, the faculty member will consider it as one more "frame" in an ongoing "movie."

mini-case studies: providing written evaluations

For each of the following situations, consider how you'd deal with the issue. Your goal is to be constructive and forward looking, while still providing a clear record that you've addressed the concern in case the desired level of progress doesn't occur.

○ ○ ○

One faculty member has become too closely associated with the program that he or she leads. There have been frequent references to "my program" and "my teaching assistants," which are creating difficulties with the other professors in the area. Even worse, the faculty member has become so close to the program that he or she is having a hard time delegating responsibilities to others and takes professional disagreements personally. Students in the discipline have sometimes expressed their concern about working on projects with different advisors because they're afraid this faculty member will be "offended" and retaliate. You don't have any clear evidence that this sort of retaliation has occurred but you'd like to address the problem before matters reach that point.

○ ○ ○

Another faculty member is a tenured full professor who is widely regarded as an ineffective teacher. Peer evaluations have noted that the professor lectures when more active learning strategies would be more appropriate,

(Continued)

moves far too rapidly in introductory courses for the students to master the material, and often cannot be understood because of a thick accent. (English is not the faculty member's native language.) The faculty member is no longer productive in research, not an effective grant writer, and not distinguished in any other way that your institution regards as important for his or her position. If the faculty member were not yet tenured, you would not hesitate to recommend nonrenewal, but that option isn't open to you. You want to include some specific recommendations about how the faculty member can improve, although you suspect that he or she is too far advanced in his or her career to be open to much change or time-consuming pedagogical workshops.

○ ○ ○

A third faculty member has a curriculum vitae that initially looks quite impressive until you explore it in greater detail. The evaluation standards at your institution regard peer-reviewed publications as a highly desirable indicator of effective research, and criteria for adequate progress are established in terms of the number of publications for which the individual is sole or first author. This faculty member more than meets the requirement to be evaluated as outstanding in research, but his or her publications, although peer-reviewed, are incredibly brief (often less than a single page), placed in undistinguished journals, and related to issues that members of the discipline often regard as insufficiently academic in nature. University policy requires you to rate the faculty member as an "outstanding" researcher, even though you regard his or her work as mediocre at best, and you'd like the professor's scholarship to improve in future years.

○ combining oral and written reviews into a comprehensive evaluation

Most written evaluations do not occur in isolation. They're usually combined with an oral review that allows the faculty member to ask questions and challenge items in the evaluation that seem unjustified, while giving the reviewer an opportunity to provide a bit more detail or background to the written remarks. That's an extremely useful approach since both oral and written processes have their own advantages and limitations. Combining these two forms of review into a truly comprehensive process helps to overcome the limitations that are inherent in one approach while preserving its benefits.

As an example, a university's regulations may require that open-ended comments on a written evaluation be kept to a certain length or address only certain issues. The oral follow-up then allows the reviewer to provide the amount of detail that's not possible due to space limitations or to expand on various positive aspects of the person's performance. For instance, as part of a promotion evaluation, a reviewer might say, "Even though our policies restrict the evaluation of service to contributions made within your academic discipline, I want to express how much I personally appreciate all the work you've done for the county's United Way campaign. Although achievements like that can't appear in the written report and don't affect the results of your evaluations, I do value them personally as your colleague." Notice that this type of amplification is possible only in areas where you're discussing someone's positive performance.

If you begin to address an area of low achievement that's not directly relevant to the criteria and standards of the evaluation, you're moving into territory that could easily result in an appeal or grievance. In other words, oral reviews can clarify concerns that have already been mentioned in the written report, but shouldn't deviate too far into new areas of criticism, even if the goal is merely to provide some good advice. Leave those recommendations for a later mentoring session when it will be clear to the faculty member that these suggestions are not to be considered a part of his or her formal evaluation.

mini-case studies: how to combine oral and written evaluations

Imagine that colleagues from several different institutions are asking you for advice about some challenges they're facing. Each challenge refers to an issue arising from a comprehensive oral and written evaluation. What do you recommend in each case?

○ ○ ○

The first colleague is having trouble with a tenure review that's taking place in his or her area. Your colleague wants to issue a negative recommendation, but each written annual evaluation the faculty member has received in the past stated that his or her performance was satisfactory, at times even very good.

At first, you think the solution is clear. You want to tell your colleague, "You need to talk to the person who wrote those evaluations. That's where the problem lies. Who was that?" Your colleague then replies, "I wrote them." When you ask why there's such a disparity between his or her conclusions on the annual evaluations and what he or she wants to recommend now, the response is, "Well, there are a couple of factors at play here. To begin with, each year's performance when you look at it in isolation was satisfactory or better: it technically met our criteria for an acceptable performance. But when we evaluate someone for tenure, we have to consider the candidate's likelihood of continued progress as a teacher and scholar based on the pattern of his or her work to date. And when you view the portfolio from that perspective, it just doesn't add up. There hasn't been a record of progress. Second, it's not that I never discussed these issues with the faculty member. In addition to providing a written evaluation, I always had a one-on-one meeting afterward to go over my concerns. And it was in those meetings that I noted the lack of adequate progress that I was seeing. We must've had conversations of this sort at least four or five times."

What do you tell your colleague to do in the current situation? Can a negative tenure decision still be justified? What advice do you provide your friend about avoiding similar problems in the future?

○ ○ ○

The second colleague is dealing with a faculty member who always complains that his or her written evaluations aren't positive enough. If the reviewer states that the professor's performance was good in some area, he or she insists that this conclusion be changed to "very good." If the evaluation has been that the professor's performance was very good, the professor wants the result to be expressed as "excellent," and so on. "I can't tell you how much time gets wasted on these petty issues," your colleague tells you. "This particular faculty member is so aggressive and such a nuisance about it that I usually do end up changing a few of my statements in the evaluation just to make the complaining stop. I mean, you have no idea what this person's modus operandi has been: writing letters to the local newspaper, contacting our governing board, speaking out in the faculty senate, and basically stirring things up in every possible way. Now I'm in the midst of a new evaluation, and I don't know what to do. Should I state my honest opinion and then have to deal with all the weeks of arguments and grievances that will inevitably result? Or should I score this professor one category lower than I really believe to be appropriate and let allow myself to be 'talked into' one ranking higher, basically resulting in the category I really wanted all along?"

What alternatives might you provide to address your colleague's predicament? How might he or she combine oral and written processes in an effective way to reduce this problem, even if it can't be eliminated altogether?

o o o

Your third call has to do with discrepancies between two sets of records. "I've got this faculty member who's a real pain," your friend begins, "abrasive, suspicious, unsociable, and constantly disruptive in meetings. A terrible colleague. As if that weren't bad enough, there isn't much I can point to that's been successful in this person's record. Teaching, scholarship, service—everything is weak right across the board. There's absolutely nothing redeeming about this person." "Is the faculty member tenured?" you ask. "Of course! Otherwise I would've dealt with this problem long ago. Anyway, just over a year ago, this faculty member applied for a job at another university more than five hundred miles away. Seeing this as a chance to get rid of a disaster, I wrote an absolutely glowing letter of recommendation. I thought I could get that other school to hire our problem and improve our area. But as you can imagine, the interview didn't go well, and that other job never materialized.

(Continued)

Now here's my big problem: somehow the faculty member got a copy of my letter. I have to deal with a grievance filed against me because my review was so positive in that letter of recommendation but strongly negative in an evaluation I wrote only a few days later."

The faculty member has claimed in the grievance that the reviewer has always been highly impressed by his or her work (and so didn't want to lie to a valued colleague at the other school) but internally has been doing everything possible to prevent the faculty member from being promoted or receiving a merit increase due to jealousy, resentment, and discrimination. The faculty member is also claiming that the reviewer had been much more positive in oral evaluations than when putting matters into writing, even though neither of them can prove precisely what was said in those meetings.

How do you help your friend deal with this complex problem?

○ conclusion

Although it may be college or university policy that certain types of reviews must be conducted orally, while others have to be in writing, it's clear that both of these approaches have certain limitations. For this reason, if institutional policy permits, reviewers can be well served by complementing an oral evaluation with a written follow-up, or vice versa. For many reasons, the best possible way of providing this type of comprehensive review is to begin the process by having the faculty member assemble a portfolio that contains raw data, interpretations, and conclusions from those data, accompanying this information with plans for the future. Those three sources of information can then be discussed with the faculty member, with a follow-up memo formalizing the conclusions of that meeting. We'll explore this portfolio approach to review and evaluation in greater detail in Chapters Eleven and Twelve.

References

Buller, J. L. (2006). *The essential department chair: A practical guide to college adminis-tration*. San Francisco: Jossey-Bass/Anker.

Grote, R. C. (1996). *The complete guide to performance appraisal.* New York: AMACOM.

Herold, D. M., Parsons, C. K., & Rensvold, R. B. (1996). Individual differences in the generation and processing of performance feedback. *Educational and Psychological Measurement, 56*(1), 5–25.

Ivancevich, J. M., Konopaske, R., & Matteson, M. T. (2010). *Organizational behavior and management.* New York: McGraw-Hill.

O'Brien, L. (2000). Added evaluation: Improving performance appraisal interviews. *Supply Management, 5*(9), 36–37.

Van Fleet, D. D., Peterson, T. O., & Van Fleet, E. W. (2005). Closing the performance feedback gap with expert systems. *Academy of Management Executive, 19*(3), 38–53.

part two

primarily formative review and evaluation

4

annual performance appraisals and evaluations

Nearly every college or university requires some type of annual performance review. Some systems don't offer tenure, while others preserve only a single rank for all members of the faculty and thus have no need for promotion evaluations. Some faculty members aren't eligible for certain distinctions because they're part-time or not on a tenure track. Posttenure review has not yet been implemented at certain institutions, and some have fixed salary scales that make merit increase evaluations unnecessary. But annual reviews of some sort can be found at institutions regardless of whether they're public or private, for-profit or non-profit, virtual or traditional.

The purpose of the review is usually formative and aimed at ongoing improvement of performance, although as we'll see in Chapter Seven it's common practice to combine these evaluations with determination of merit salary increases. These annual reviews may be highly structured and used to determine whether the person's employment will continue, or they may consist of little more than an informal conversation about that person's performance during the past year, but it's the rare college or university that doesn't require at least a nominal review of a faculty member's work on an annual basis. Indeed, for department chairs, the annual review may be the only type of evaluation they conduct by themselves, with all others handled either by a committee, a higher-level administrator, or an office of human resources. For this reason, it's appropriate that we give particularly careful consideration to best practices in performing these evaluations and avoiding common mistakes.

We'll follow the distinction that was established in Chapter One, with the term *appraisals* referring to the judgment a supervisor makes about how well an employee (usually a staff member) is performing the duties outlined in his or her job description and the term *evaluations* referring to summative reviews that determine whether someone's performance has met certain standards. For this reason, we'll treat performance appraisals as largely in the domain of the office of human resources and thus primarily a matter that concerns the staff, and we'll consider performance evaluations as falling in the domain of academic affairs and thus primarily a matter that concerns the faculty. That distinction may be somewhat artificial in certain situations, but adopting it for our purposes offers a shorthand way of referring to what type of employee is affected by the review and which division of the university sets those policies. Also, since the focus of this book is on faculty reviews and evaluations, most of this chapter explores performance evaluations, concluding with a brief look at performance appraisals so that their major differences are clear.

○ offering constructive criticism

Although annual performance evaluations can conclude with summative judgments, they're often far less structured than tenure, promotion, or posttenure reviews. In many cases, the chair, director, or dean alone conducts the evaluation, although sometimes his or her supervisor has to sign off on the result. Despite their common informality, most institutional policies expect that annual reviews will highlight recognition of the faculty member's achievements and areas where improvement has occurred, identification of areas where further progress is still necessary, and guidance about how the person could improve.

In offering this type of constructive criticism, it's useful to observe several important principles. First, remember the basic review framework that was established in Chapter One: you can't evaluate someone effectively without knowing the purpose of the evaluation. So go over your institution's or program's policies on annual reviews in order to have in mind what type of constructive criticism you should provide and what type of issues are irrelevant. Second, make it clear from both your tone and your language that you are trying to be helpful, not merely pointing out flaws for their own sake or laying the groundwork for a negative personnel decision. It's not merely junior faculty members who may interpret a mild suggestion by a chair, dean, or provost as a severe indictment of his or her entire performance. Faculty members vary widely in their sensitivity to criticism, and the distinguished senior scholar who has nothing at all to worry about regarding his or her future at the institution may shock you by being the very person who seems crushed by your mildest, most helpful suggestion. The goal, then, is to make certain that constructive criticism is clearly presented as a desire to be helpful and that careful consideration is always given to the needs and personalities of the people you're reviewing.

The third principle to keep in mind is that it's useful to cite some concrete examples of the type of activity you're hoping the faculty member can improve. But provide only a few of these. If you're not specific about what the faculty member did that could benefit from further attention, he or she may not be able to see the connection between the advice you're try to provide and his or her own practices or behavior. But if you offer an entire litany of instances where the faculty member failed to live up to expected standards, the point you're trying to make will become lost in this welter of criticism. "Rather than write down all those occasions when I didn't meet your 'expectations,'" the faculty member may ask, "why didn't you just come and talk to me? Why is now the first time that I'm hearing about these issues?" And the faculty member is probably right. You should develop the habit of offering praise and noting areas of improvement as you notice them. But both in those situations and during an annual review, be judicious about the number of instances you cite when you're offering criticism. People are usually less defensive when you keep the examples few, concrete, and focused on the behavior itself, not the person involved.

Let's suppose for a moment that you have a very successful faculty member who comes across as blunt or abrasive in faculty meetings. The result is that other members of the program are reluctant to serve on the same committees or discuss research ideas with this professor. You might phrase your recommendations with some variation of the following:

> As usual, everything you've done in the areas of teaching and research this past year has been absolutely first rate. And we'll be celebrating some instances of those successes in a moment. But one thing that I would like to mention is a way in which we might be able to get the department to work together a bit more constructively. You've got a very quick insight into where the weakest points of a proposal are likely to be. And many times that's extremely helpful. But sometimes it seems as though in your effort to dispose of impractical suggestions quickly, your remarks may come across as abrupt or even condescending. I think other people just need a little more time to absorb and consider other people's remarks than you do. For example, at the graduate curriculum meeting in March, when Blaine presented the suggestion to merge the M.A. and M.S. programs in order to save resources, what I witnessed was that you came on so quickly and so aggressively that Blaine just shut down immediately. My concern is that even if the idea was flawed, we ought to consider every proposal because of the pending budget cut, and now Blaine is reluctant to say anything in any meeting where you're present.
>
> Let's see if we can't find a way for you to get your thoughts and insights across, but in a more constructive and helpful way that can keep our meetings positive. That'll help bring your level of leadership in those areas up to the spectacular work you do in teaching and research. And speaking of those areas, what has been particularly impressive about your performance is . . .

The fourth thing to remember while offering constructive criticism is to provide specific suggestions for improvement, not merely concerns about what needs to be changed. It's not very helpful to say, "You haven't performed enough service this year," unless you clarify what would have been a sufficient level of service and how the faculty member can reach that level next year. Offering specific advice is important for every faculty member, but it's absolutely essential in the case of probationary faculty members who are yet to be considered for tenure or a multiyear contract. Reviewers need to provide a frank and accurate assessment of the faculty member's level of performance that year, whether he or she is on track for tenure or the next major personnel decision, and what steps he or she can take in order to do even better next year.

When looking at the faculty member's career path, it's important to understand that annual progress and overall progress are not necessarily the same. For example, let's imagine a hypothetical institution where tenure decisions are made following six years of full-time service and where five peer-reviewed research publications are regarded as the absolute minimum for a positive decision. If you're evaluating a faculty member in his or her fifth year and you see that the faculty member has had three major articles accepted for publication that year in first-tier journals, your annual evaluation of this person's research is likely to be extremely favorable. But if the faculty member had published nothing, made no conference presentations, and not even demonstrated progress in collecting data during the preceding four years, your overall evaluation of the faculty member's progress is likely to be more negative. If you're the person's chair or mentor, the time has come to discuss candidly what the faculty member's career plan should be. Is it still possible to turn this situation around so the faculty member can make the type of progress that will lead to a positive outcome? If so, what steps should this person take, and what resources may be available to help him or her? If the situation is already hopeless, has the faculty member developed a backup plan, and what does he or she need to do to be in the best position to take advantage of other opportunities?

The final principle is that even in the case of constructive criticism, people often need time to process the advice they've received. Don't be surprised if the faculty member returns later and requests a follow-up conversation. Most of these subsequent discussions will begin with a question like, "What exactly did you mean when you said that I should . . . ?" In these cases, the faculty member has moved from processing the nature of your advice to considering exactly how to implement it. These subsequent conversations provide useful opportunities to reiterate key points of your suggestions, offer more specific guidance, and develop a reasonable plan to reach the goals you've set forth. Far less pleasant can be the conversations where the faculty member becomes preoccupied with the small number of minor suggestions you made during an otherwise positive annual review and now wants to dispute them.

Wounded egos occur in all walks of life, but they appear to be particularly common in higher education. We've all had the experience of reading through a stack of extremely positive student course evaluations, finding one that is marginally less positive, and then losing track of everything pleasant the students said because we can't get that one unsatisfying remark out of our heads. Constructive criticism can affect faculty members in precisely this way. If someone appears to be fixated on the negative, your best approach may be to reiterate the predominantly positive message you had intended to convey, clarify that your suggestion was not a criticism but advice on how to make a good performance even better, and engage the faculty member in a more forward-looking exchange about how to build on past successes.

mini-case studies: offering constructive criticism

Since you've been so successful in conducting faculty evaluations, a young department chair seeks your advice on how to handle each of the following situations. What advice would you provide to your colleague in each of these situations?

o   o   o

One member of the chair's department is a very distinguished senior scholar and researcher. To complicate matters, that professor was once the chair's own mentor when he or she was a student. Despite the professor's great distinction, there are some pedagogical techniques that he or she hasn't kept up with that students expect today, and their evaluations increasingly reflect this problem.

How can the chair provide constructive criticism in a manner that demonstrates respect for the professor's distinguished status and overcomes the awkwardness that might result from how their roles have changed over the years?

o o o

Another member of the department is only a few years younger than the chair. But this faculty member has demonstrated anxiety about his or her eventual tenure review that at times nearly borders on panic.

How can the chair provide the constructive advice this faculty member needs to hear in his or her annual review without either stoking this person's paranoia or suggesting that "everything's going to work out fine" when the outcome of the tenure decision is still a number of years away?

o o o

A third member of the chair's department is performing extremely well in all areas relevant to the current evaluation. Nevertheless, the faculty member regularly neglects matters of personal hygiene, with the result that others in the discipline are unwilling to work closely with this professor, serve on the same committees, or recommend the professor for important recognitions that—on paper, at least—he or she would probably receive. The chair can find nothing in the institutional handbook or guidelines that can be used as a basis for addressing this type of problem during an annual review. Nevertheless, the chair believes that this matter has become a major professional impediment for the faculty member.

Does the chair have the right to mention this matter as constructive advice during the faculty member's annual review? If so, how should the matter be addressed? If not, how should chair handle this issue?

○ offering praise and recognition

While providing constructive criticism can be difficult, many people find that offering praise and recognition is almost as challenging. For some reviewers, spending time indulging in compliments and accolades makes them uncomfortable and doesn't seem to fit their gruff or introverted personalities. For others, it can seem a waste of time to talk about what's going right when fixing what's wrong seems more important. Still others fully understand that recognizing excellent work is important, but they can never figure out ways to express these thoughts beyond variations of, "Good job at A, B, and C, by the way." And yet offering praise and recognition can be the most critical part of the annual evaluation. It helps soften any criticism you may provide, calls attention to behavior you'd like to see repeated in the future, and offers a powerful motivation for faculty members to do their very best for the program and institution. If that weren't enough, recognizing the good work of employees and taking steps to increase their overall job satisfaction have repeatedly been shown to be far more effective than criticism in improving performance. (See, for example, Gomez-Mejia, 1990; Wiley, 1997; Luthans, 2000; and Harter, Schmidt, and Hayes, 2002.) So there are excellent reasons why even reviewers who love to offer praise and recognition may wish to become even more effective in doing so in order to see the full effects of this powerful motivational tool.

We saw earlier that it's very important to provide clear, specific examples when offering criticism. That advice is equally true when offering praise and recognition. A general statement like, "Your teaching was really great this year," has neither the impact nor the value of such phrasing as, "The way in which the students in your research methods course prepared their proposals and outlines when they got to our senior seminar was truly outstanding. It was obvious to everyone that they had really mastered how to refine their research questions, conduct thorough literature reviews, and take advantage of recent discoveries. They led the class in understanding how to identify the most relevant sources and apply the appropriate analytical methods to the data. If you have a chance, I'd like you to mentor some of our graduate students who are preparing for university careers. They could really benefit from the teaching techniques you've used." Expressed in this way, your praise achieves five objectives simultaneously.

1. It indicates that you're not just offering a compliment simply because it's expected of you. It's obvious from your remarks that you know exactly what the professor did and understand why those achievements are important.

2. It stresses the impact of the faculty member's contribution. Your comments answer the question, "Why was this professor's success as an instructor important?" or simply, "Why did all of that hard work matter?" Emphasizing the significance of an accomplishment is important for sustaining motivation during times when the challenges are huge and the faculty member's sense of frustration may be increasing.

3. It takes time to let the person being reviewed take in either positive or negative news. Brief statements like, "Good job on that grant proposal," are better than nothing, but they don't have much of an effect. By the time the person realizes that he or she is being praised, it's over and you're on to the next subject.

4. It tells the faculty member exactly what he or she did that was praiseworthy and makes it clear that you'd like to see that type of behavior continue. The faculty member leaves the evaluation session with a clear idea of what to do next year.

5. It links the faculty member's good work to programmatic goals. By requesting (though not insisting) that the professor share his or her insights with current graduate students, you reinforce your own goal of better preparing tomorrow's teachers in what their actual duties will be, offer the faculty member an opportunity for even greater recognition, and underscore how truly significant you believe his or her accomplishment was.

In sum, there are four basic guidelines to follow when offering praise and recognition:

1. *Be as specific as possible.* General recognitions like, "Thank you for all you've done," have very little impact.

2. *Cite examples of the faculty member's superior performance* so that he or she will understand exactly what to do more of in the future.

3. *Spend sufficient time allowing the faculty member to bask in the glow of the positive remarks that you're making.* Although excessive or fulsome praise is likely to embarrass some people, it is usually better to err on the side of offering too much rather than too little positive reinforcement.

4. *Vary the praise or recognition offered according to the needs of the faculty member.* Although the examples we're considering occur in the context of an annual review, it can often be effective to supplement formal evaluations with more informal ways of letting people know they've done well. Of course, people are different with respect to how they prefer to receive recognition. Some respond well to public recognition during a faculty meeting, while others will be embarrassed by unexpected public attention. Some will appreciate the personal touch of a handwritten note, while others will dismiss this gesture as proof that you were "too cheap to buy a card." The better you know your faculty members, the easier it will be to adapt the forms in which you provide them with this extra recognition. (For many other ideas about how to offer praise in a meaningful manner, see Nelson, 2005.)

---

mini-case studies: offering praise and recognition

You're reviewing a faculty member who believes he or she is grossly under-paid when compared to others with the same qualifications and level of experience in the discipline. Your own examination of the facts suggests that there is no real discrepancy and that the faculty member has merely cherry-picked data that support his or her argument. Every time in the past that you have offered praise during this faculty member's annual review, those statements have been used against you later. At one faculty meeting, for example, the professor read the positive remarks you included in the past three annual evaluations and said, "If I'm doing so well, why am I so underpaid?" Now you've learned that the professor plans to contact the institution's governing board and local reporters if he or she receives yet another positive evaluation that is not accompanied with a sizable salary increase. As you review the faculty member's performance for the year, you find that his or her achievements were above average, though by no means stellar.

How might you offer the recognition this faculty member deserves while decreasing the likelihood that you'll come to regret your own words later?

○ ○ ○

Another faculty member is extremely self-conscious, and you know that any form of praise or recognition, even when offered in private, tends to be counterproductive. He or she becomes even more reserved and thus demonstrates less of the behavior you admired in the first place. Your challenge is that this professor has had an absolutely phenomenal year, with outstanding achievements in teaching, research, and service that certainly qualify for a university award, perhaps even a national award. (Having a faculty member honored in this way would be highly beneficial to your programs too.)

How do you address this situation during the professor's annual review? Is there any way to reward the faculty member without causing such a shy person the sort of embarrassment that's caused problems in the past? Do you even mention the possibility of a university or national award? If so, how do you raise the issue? If not, what's your justification when your supervisor later challenges your decision not to say anything to a potential honoree?

○ ○ ○

You have a faculty member who responds extremely well to praise and positive reinforcement. Although penalties or even threats of future sanctions have not worked in the past, you've noticed that public recognition brings about a burst of excellent performance from this professor. Unfortunately, the current year has been the worst yet for this faculty member. You can identify no clear strengths or progress in any of the categories you're evaluating, and your evaluation will have to be negative.

Is there any way in which you can soften this inevitable conclusion with some type of praise or recognition, since you know that acclaim tends to motivate this faculty member? Since the professor responds particularly well to public recognition, is there any way to provide it without incurring the ridicule or anger of the rest of the faculty who are aware that the professor accomplished extremely little this year?

○ setting new annual goals

An important part of each annual review should be the establishment
of new goals for the coming year. The creation of goals should occur
in the context of a genuine dialogue, and you should be open to considering what the faculty member suggests as possible objectives. In
the end, however, it's also your responsibility as the reviewer to see
that the faculty member isn't setting the bar too low and that his or
her professional objectives align well with overall programmatic and
institutional goals. In the case of probationary faculty members, it's
important to take into account the standards the person will need to
meet in order to be successful at tenure or promotion, break those
expectations down into manageable yearly objectives, and include
those objectives as part of the faculty member's work plan for the
coming year.

Probably the best way to make these standards manageable for
faculty members is to work collaboratively with them to develop a
multiyear plan that carries them through their next major personnel
review. For probationary faculty members, this plan is most effectively
established during their orientation or as part of a faculty first-year-
experience program intended to provide mentoring and faculty development. A carefully structured multiyear plan can be the basis for each
year's annual goals, and you can end each annual (summative) evaluation with an honest but forward-looking analysis of what still needs to
be done, making the process consciously formative-summative. These
goal-setting sessions are a valuable supplement to constructive criticism
and sincere praise.

Herbert Meyer, Emanuel Kay, and John French (1965) discovered
that a collaborative effort between supervisors and employees to set
mutually acceptable goals had a far greater effect on overall performance than did either constructive criticism or praise alone (similar
results were obtained by Kim and Hamner, 1976, and Wilk and Redmon,
1998). For this reason, annual evaluation sessions can be much more
productive if you adopt a modified version of the familiar sandwich
review, where criticism occurs between supportive remarks so that the

meeting both begins and ends on a positive note. This modified or expanded structure would look something like this:

1. *Positive initial remarks.* Focus on one or more things the faculty member has done well during the past year, and indicate that this contribution was significant, noticed, and appreciated.

2. *Constructive criticism.* Move on to areas where improvement seems desirable, and discuss with the faculty member specific ways in which to address these concerns.

3. *Reiteration of the positive.* Make it clear that you have confidence that the faculty member is capable of improving in this way, and reinforce your recognition of the faculty member's achievements.

4. *Set annual goals.* Discuss specific ways in which the faculty member's achievements can be continued or increased, while any areas of concerns can be reduced, leading to a work plan for the coming year.

5. *Follow up.* A day or two later, provide the faculty member with a brief, confidential memo outlining the key points of this evaluation meeting, and retain a copy in your files.

mini-case studies: setting annual goals

As you meet with a faculty member to discuss potential goals for the coming year, how might you handle each of the following situations?

1. The faculty member proposes goals that you believe are not sufficiently challenging and don't really help advance the goal of excellent teaching and research in your program.

2. The faculty member proposes goals that are significant but don't really mesh well with the primary needs of your area. For instance, the faculty member suggests shifting his or her research focus from an emphasis in which the program has traditionally been strong (and for which this particular faculty member was hired) to a new area that you regard as far less relevant to the goals and mission of your program.

3. The faculty member sets goals that are far too ambitious and that you're certain cannot possibly be achieved within a single year.

4. The faculty member challenges you at every turn, claiming that your praise was not warm enough, your criticisms were without merit, and your recommended goals are unreasonable.

○ evaluating progress on annual goals

The copy of the follow-up memo that you keep in your files will be of significant value during the next year's review when you consider the degree to which the faculty member has achieved the annual goals you both set. Naturally the goals are designed to be a general road map for the year, not a fixed itinerary that can never be changed once it's set: opportunities will arise that weren't on the horizon a few months before, and unexpected setbacks will crop up. Because of other changes in staffing, even the specific courses that the faculty member was assigned to teach may need to be adjusted at the last moment.

Few plans are ever likely to be fulfilled precisely as they were written. Nevertheless, the previous year's goals provide a valuable framework for you to discuss the level of progress that has occurred. Everyone occasionally faces a year that proves to be far tougher than anticipated. But if a faculty member has several years in succession when he or she falls significantly short of the goals the two of you mutually agreed on, you'll have a clear opening to describe the pattern that's emerging and the likely implications it'll have on the person's next major personnel review.

If you're the faculty member's supervisor (rather than, say, a colleague assigned to an annual review committee), very little that you tell the person about his or her progress toward meeting annual goals should come as a surprise. Although, as we've seen, annual evaluations are required by most colleges and universities, there's absolutely no reason that chairs, deans, or provosts can't meet with a faculty member more frequently to identify significant achievements and develop strategies for overcoming areas of concern. These informal updates can provide the formative element that is too often missing from purely summative annual evaluations. So if the evaluation results in a judgment of inadequate progress in research or that the faculty member's teaching has not met institutional standards, the person being reviewed should already be aware that these areas were recognized as problems and have been given advice on how to improve. Furthermore, if the previous year's goals had been properly formulated—neither hopelessly vague ("Improve your teaching during the coming academic year") nor excessively detailed ("Complete at least one article of no less than three published pages that will appear in *Science*")—any objective reviewer should be able to discern whether that goal has been reached.

You don't want the evaluation to degenerate into disputes about semantics—"You *said* publish more, and my annual summary indicates that I did publish more." "Yes, but an additional twenty-seven words over an unsuccessful previous year isn't at all what I had in mind"—but you also don't want the goal you set to be so narrow that the faculty member is penalized for failing to meet the letter of the objective while more than fulfilling its spirit. Your primary concern should always be how well this faculty member achieved the purpose that was behind each goal set the previous year.

mini-case studies: reviewing annual goals

Several of your colleagues at other institutions have asked you for advice. What do you tell each of them?

o o o

One colleague works at a university that's rapidly trying to change its reputation from that of an exceptionally fine teaching institution to that of a widely recognized research university. He or she is reviewing a faculty member who didn't achieve any of the previous year's goals in the area of research but did win a prestigious national award for excellence in teaching and was recently appointed by the federal government to head a major task force on how to improve postsecondary education. Your colleague is at a loss over how to address the faculty member's simultaneous failure to meet a goal that the institution has identified as its highest priority and phenomenal success in an area that the university is deemphasizing.

What do you recommend?

o o o

(Continued)

Another colleague works at a college that has no formal tenure review process and bases salary solely on seniority without any system for awarding merit pay. He or she is reviewing a tenured full professor who consistently fails to meet the annual goals the two of them agreed on the previous year. Your colleague feels that he or she has no more carrots or sticks to motivate this faculty member, but is under pressure to make sure that all the "deadwood" in the discipline starts producing more desirable results.

Do you have any suggestions to offer your colleague?

o   o   o

A third friend is having trouble with a faculty member who clearly excels in teaching, research, and service—each year, surpassing the previous year's goals—but is creating such severe morale problems that other valued members of the program have left to work elsewhere. Although the institution doesn't consider collegiality to be a separate factor in annual reviews or when promotion and tenure decisions are being made, a serious lack of collegiality seems to lie at the heart of this faculty member's problems.

Your friend wants to know the best way to relate these collegiality issues to the ways in which his or her institution does evaluate progress on achieving annual goals. What do you recommend?

o   the formative-summative annual evaluation

Combining goal setting with formal evaluation means that annual reviews often assume a formative-summative dimension. As such, it will be important to clarify which findings fall into which of these two categories in the written report that the faculty member receives or during the evaluation meeting itself. If you don't make this distinction, you can easily find yourself confusing the faculty member who's under review and being asked such questions as, "But how can you hold it against me for not working more closely with a research mentor? You only told me about that program today." It may seem perfectly clear to you which of your statements are intended to be evaluative judgments and which are simply constructive advice for the future, but that difference can become unclear to the faculty member you're reviewing.

In oral evaluations, it's often useful to begin with a statement like, "I'd like to break our meeting today into two parts. In the first part, we're going to review your performance over the past year, and I'm going to provide you with my evaluation of that performance in each of the areas relevant to this review. Then in the second part, we're going to move beyond that evaluation of past performance to set some goals for the coming year, discuss any factors you feel might explain any weaknesses I've mentioned, and end by considering a few ways in which you can do even better in the future. Is that distinction between the two halves of our meeting clear?" In a similar way, written evaluations should visibly divide summative evaluation from formative advice through sections clearly labeled something like "Evaluation of Past Achievements" and "Recommendations for Future Goals." Anyone reading the document should have no doubt about which statements relate to past performance and which are intended as guidance for future growth.

The summative part of a formative-summative evaluation should be tied directly to the written standards and criteria for evaluation, as straightforward as possible in its conclusion, and based on both achievements occurring during the review period itself and the pattern of progress you've noticed over time. When you identify that pattern of progress, you might include such statements as, "As I look at your overall performance, therefore, you continue to be on track for tenure and promotion at the designated time," or, "The significant decline in research this past year is clearly a deviation from your usual pattern of excellence in this area and will need to be rectified next year."

The formative part of the evaluation can focus on any areas of weakness you noted during your summative remarks, methods of improving performance that are mere suggestions rather than absolute requirements, or both. For example, if you decided that a faculty member was unsatisfactory in service while you were drawing your summative conclusions, your formative recommendation might be that he or she work with a mentor who has been creative in developing new service activities and express to colleagues his or her willingness to serve on major committees.

Helpful advice not directly related to the standards and criteria of the evaluation can be made, but make it clear that you're only offering a suggestion, not attempting to penalize the faculty member. For instance, you might recommend that a faculty member sit more centrally in departmental meetings rather than constantly remaining at the back of the room, so that he or she can become more involved in discussions. Although no one would ever base an evaluation on something as trivial as where a faculty member chooses to sit during a meeting, you may still wish to underscore where your role as an evaluator ends and your role as a mentor begins.

○ annual performance appraisals for the staff

As the title of this book says, our focus is on faculty reviews and evaluations. Nevertheless, since many administrators are required to evaluate staff members as well, it may be useful to point out a few ways in which that process differs from a faculty review. As we saw in Chapter One, staff members usually undergo a performance appraisal (even if the institution refers to it as a review or evaluation), which can differ significantly from the process used with faculty.

First, performance appraisals are usually conducted by the person's supervisor alone, while faculty evaluations often contain at least some 360-degree information from students and peers as well, even if it comes only in the form of data drawn from student course evaluations. Second, performance appraisals focus largely on the individual's own classification and job description, while faculty evaluations, regardless of title, are usually based on some version of the standard academic triad (teaching, research, and service). In the staff member's formal job classification, as established by the person's supervisor or the office of human resources, there are probably several specific duties listed—for example:

• Provide administrative support to the department, including but not limited to general clerical work, scheduling meetings, maintaining calendars and files, and making travel arrangements.

- Establish priorities so as to complete all assigned duties in a timely manner.
- Order lab supplies as necessary in accordance with institutional purchasing guidelines.
- Anticipate clerical or administrative problems, taking appropriate actions to solve them.

The appraisal process thus involves determining the degree to which these assigned duties were carried out and the quality of the work that resulted. In the case of clearly unsatisfactory work, the office of human resources has a number of options—such as reclassification, reassignment, retraining, or termination—that may differ from those available when reviewing faculty members. As a result, it is almost always the case that faculty evaluations and staff appraisals follow entirely different procedures, even if the same person is in charge of conducting both of them. (For a more complete discussion of staff performance appraisals and how they differ from faculty reviews, see Grote, 1996.)

○ conclusion

Simply because you're conducting evaluations of faculty members annually doesn't mean that you need to wait that long when a major issue arises. You're much more likely to increase that person's level of performance and the reputation of your area if you provide immediate recognition for someone's accomplishments and share that information with the upper administration. At the same time, don't wait to intervene when there are cases of inappropriate behavior, since you may be appearing to condone it, and even small problems can become catastrophes if left unaddressed. If you're in doubt, seek legal counsel or consult with your supervisor about the most effective way to handle inappropriate behavior as soon as you become aware of it. Particularly if you're a dean or department chair, your best approach may be to establish a culture of providing informal feedback so that when a problem needs to be addressed, it is viewed as part of your standard operating procedure, not a situation in which the faculty member is being singled out for criticism and punishment.

Greg Martin (2007), director of international business programs at the University of West Florida, identifies four key steps to follow in every type of faculty review:

Step One: Clearly define the criteria by which the person is being evaluated. These criteria should always be set in advance through an objective process and known to the person being reviewed. Criteria that are established ad hoc, perhaps because they can be used to penalize or dismiss someone, are unfair to the faculty member, contrary to the long-term interests of the institution, and quite likely to make successful appeals and lawsuits more probable.

Step Two: Establish well-defined performance standards expectations for each criterion. In other words, it's not enough to say that a faculty member will be evaluated for excellence in teaching, research, and service. What constitutes excellence in each of these areas? Institutions and programs must identify the information on which they will base these judgments and the expectations they have for each standard. Those expectations must be realistic, measurable, and unambiguous. We return to this topic in greater detail in Chapter Ten.

Step Three: Create descriptors that indicate the level of performance that was achieved. As discussed in Chapter Two, those descriptors may be numerical (such as on a scale of 1 to 5), verbal (such as Outstanding to Unsatisfactory), or some other scale that's appropriate to the discipline. In all cases, the approach used should result in a definitive judgment about the quality of the faculty member's performance.

Step Four: Integrate other relevant reporting requirements into the annual evaluation. For instance, if the faculty member is probationary, how well does that year's performance reflect adequate progress toward tenure and promotion? If the faculty member is tenured, how do the person's achievements position the faculty member for the next post-tenure review?

Annual evaluations can require a significant investment of time for most administrators. If these evaluations are done poorly, that time is wasted, morale suffers, and the needed improvements don't occur. And if they're done effectively, annual evaluations can be an important part of a program's strategy to take better advantage of its strengths and address its weaknesses. They can also provide the basis for probationary pretenure and posttenure reviews, the topics we'll explore in the next two chapters.

References

Gomez-Mejia, L. R. (1990). Increasing productivity: Performance appraisal and reward systems. *Personnel Review, 19*(2), 21–26.

Grote, R. C. (1996). *The complete guide to performance appraisal.* New York: AMACOM.

Harter, J. K., Schmidt, F. L., & Hayes, T. L. (2002). Business-unit-level relationship between employee satisfaction, employee engagement, and business outcomes: A meta-analysis. *Journal of Applied Psychology, 87,* 268–79.

Kim, J. S., & Hamner, W. C. (1976). Effect of performance feedback and goal setting on productivity and satisfaction in an organizational setting. *Journal of Applied Psychology, 61*(1), 48–57.

Luthans, K. (2000). Recognition: A powerful, but often overlooked, leadership tool to improve employee performance. *Journal of Leadership and Organizational Studies, 7*(1), 31–39.

Martin, G. (2007). *Faculty evaluation: The second most important chairly task.* Retrieved from ispa.fsu.edu/ial/presentations/chairs/2007PerformanceEvaluation.ppt.

Meyer, H. H., Kay, E., & French, J.R.P. (1965). Split roles in performance appraisal. *Harvard Business Review, 43,* 123–129.

Nelson, B. (2005). *1001 ways to reward employees.* New York: Workman.

Wiley, C. (1997). What motivates employees according to over 40 years of motivation surveys. *International Journal of Manpower, 18,* 263–280.

Wilk, L. A., & Redmon, W. K. (1998). The effects of feedback and goal setting on the productivity and satisfaction of university admissions staff. *Journal of Organizational Behavior Management, 18*(1), 45–68.

Resources

Buller, J. L. (2004) Tips for conducting effective faculty evaluation sessions. *Department Chair, 14*(3), 5–8.

Hardre, P., & Cox, M. (2009). Evaluating faculty work: Expectations and standards of faculty performance in research universities. *Research Papers in Education, 24,* 383–419.

Yao, Y., & Grady, M. (2005). How do faculty make formative use of student evaluation feedback?: A multiple case study. *Journal of Personnel Evaluation in Education, 18,* 107–126.

5

probationary period pretenure reviews

Probationary period pretenure reviews—sometimes known as second- or third-year reviews—are midpoint checks to determine the progress of a recently hired faculty member. The goal is to determine whether that faculty member is performing at a level that is likely to lead to tenure or a multiyear contract at the appropriate time. These reviews necessarily have both summative and formative components. Their summative component consists of determining whether the faculty member is capable of producing a record of achievement strong enough to merit a positive decision in the time remaining. In this case, the evaluation results in an up-or-out decision. Their formative component consists of providing faculty members with guidance on how to improve if they do indeed seem on track for a successful tenure review. In that case, the evaluation results in collegial advice and criticism.

As we saw in Chapter One, formative-summative assessments always have to be approached with special care; it's easy for advice to be misconstrued as a judgment and vice versa. For this reason, the reviewer who is in charge of a probationary period pretenure process needs to be fully aware of institutional policies, established best practices, and the legal implications of the various decisions made. It's sometimes felt that a second- or third-year review is much less formal than the process involved in an official evaluation for promotion or tenure. Nevertheless, this early review can have even more significant repercussions than those later procedures, and so the entire procedure must be approached with a great deal of preparation and attention to detail.

In certain ways, the very existence of the probationary period pre-tenure review is an outgrowth of the accountability culture prevalent in higher education. Until the 1980s, pretenure evaluations were rela-tively rare. Faculty members were evaluated as part of the hiring process and then not subjected to a formal review again until consideration for tenure. Annual reviews, if they occurred at all, tended to be casual performance appraisals conducted by the chair or a senior faculty member with very little involvement of students, faculty peers, or other stakeholders. But just as the tendency to move away from basing a student's grade solely on the final exam or paper led to the proliferation of midterms and unit tests, so did the pretenure review result from a desire to provide faculty members with helpful advice while there was still time to take advantage of it. In addition, six or seven years can be a very long time for programs to endure a faculty member who is unproductive, uncooperative, or ineffective in the classroom. Although institutions always have the right to forgo renewal of a probationary faculty member's annual contract for any reason or for no reason what-soever, in practice many colleges or universities are reluctant to take so drastic a step without some type of in-depth review of the person's progress.

For all these reasons, conducting a review in a faculty member's second or third year of full-time service has proved to be a convenient way of improving the quality of instruction and research, providing faculty members with constructive advice, and cutting ties with those for whom there was little or no possibility that later evaluations would be successful.

○ considerations resulting from the summative nature of probationary reviews

These fundamental questions must be asked and answered during any probationary review:

1. Is the faculty member making adequate progress so that the result of the eventual evaluation for tenure, promotion, or multiple-year contracts is likely to be positive?
2. If the faculty member is making adequate progress, what advice can be given so as to increase his or her likelihood of success even more?
3. If the faculty member is not making adequate progress, can the situation be substantially improved by the time of that future evaluation?
4. If it can be improved, what recommendations should be given to the faculty member so as to make a positive evaluation more likely?
5. If it cannot be improved, what actions should be taken now?

As they appear on this list, the odd-numbered questions are the summative elements of the review; the even-numbered questions are the formative elements. Let's begin by considering how you should go about answering the summative questions.

Is the faculty member making adequate progress so that the result of the eventual evaluation for tenure, promotion, or multiple-year contracts is likely to be positive?
The key focus of this question—an issue that department chairs or review committees sometimes forget—is not whether the faculty member deserves to be tenured, promoted, or offered a multiyear contract now. It's whether that positive result appears to be probable in the future if his or her progress continues at the current rate.

You may be reviewing a faculty member whose evaluations for teaching by students and peers are nowhere near the minimal standard required for a positive tenure recommendation or whose production of articles in peer-reviewed publications significantly lags behind that of recently successful applicants for promotion. That single data point doesn't tell you very much. The key follow-up questions have to be: In which direction is the faculty member's work trending; and then, What is he or she doing about it? In other words, if the person being reviewed has not yet met the required standard for excellence in teaching, do the evaluations each term seem to be getting better or worse? If they're getting better, what will they be like two to four years from now if the current rates of improvement continue? If they're not getting better, what pattern are you noticing: no change at all, an improvement in some courses but not in others, a decline during some semesters but a rise during others, or a consistent decline? Most important of all, what is the faculty member doing if it's clear that improvement is needed? Is he or she working with a mentor, participating in workshops offered by a center for excellence in teaching, sitting in on the courses offered by master teachers, or doing anything at all that demonstrates a serious commitment to improving?

Similarly, in the area of research, what is the context for any progress or stagnation? Is the person completing a number of scholarly projects begun with a research team in graduate school but not yet engaging in independent scholarship or developing ties to a new research team? Is the person submitting grant applications or manuscripts for articles that are not being accepted, or is there very little record that even serious efforts have been under way? In his advice to faculty members, Robert Diamond (2004), president of the National Academy for Academic Leadership, provides some good advice about what review committees will probably be looking for when they evaluate research:

Establishing Quality

- Expert testimony such as formal reviews, juries, and solicited testimony
- A faculty essay describing the process that was followed, the rationale behind the decisions that were made, and the quality of the products

- Formal reports and studies
- Publications, displays, or videorecorded presentations

Establishing Significance

- A faculty essay explaining why the work is important, to whom, and for what purposes
- External reviews that describe the importance and value of the scholarly activity
- Impact on the intended audience: size and scope and documentation of changes in learning, attitudes, and performance
- Relation to the mission statement of the institution or department
- Documentation of individual assignment in accordance with what the department requires

These issues become particularly important in a probationary review because focus on the impact of the candidate's research can lead you to ask, "What is this faculty member's application for tenure, promotion, or a multiple-year contract likely to look like in a few years, and will that application meet our standards at that time?"

In answering these questions, it's frequently necessary for you as the reviewer to derive your insights from a large number of sources, only some of which may be provided by the faculty member as part of the application. For example, faculty members themselves may not have access to the opinions of all senior faculty in the discipline as to the appropriateness of their methods and strategies in teaching or research. They may not be aware of comparable levels of achievement reached by faculty members in related disciplines who later went on to submit successful applications for tenure, promotion, or extended contracts. They may not know how the nature of their specific assignment—such as the teaching of highly unpopular, required courses or a research agenda that will require significant groundwork before producing results—makes their situation different from that of other probationary faculty members.

The chair of the review committee thus has an important opportunity, or perhaps an obligation, to place these matters into their appropriate context at the very beginning of the process. Remember too that the goal of this particular summative evaluation is to consider levels of progress made since the faculty member was hired. As a result, single, nonrepeatable accomplishments or achievements that occurred before hiring are likely not to matter as much as the faculty member's overall pattern of performance unless those achievements were themselves sufficient to make promotion or tenure inevitable. In other words, receipt of "just one" Nobel Prize is far different from the publication of "just one" book of research, particularly if that book is largely based on the person's dissertation.

If the faculty member is not making adequate progress, can the situation be substantially improved by the time of that future evaluation? And if the situation cannot be improved, what actions should be taken now?
These questions involve the most critical summative decision that has to be made during the probationary pretenure evaluation. Notice once again that the question is not, "Is the application strong enough for approval *now*?" but rather, "Does it seem likely that the application *can become* strong enough by the time the more significant evaluation must occur?" If the answer to the second question is no, then some important decisions have to be made. As you make these decisions, keep in mind the following two unwritten rules about higher education administration:

Unwritten rule #1: The longer someone in a probationary position is allowed to remain part of a process, the greater will be his or her expectation that the outcome will ultimately be positive, and thus the greater will be his or her disappointment and anger if the outcome is negative.

Unwritten rule #2: As a result of rule #1, when it is apparent that the performance of a member of the faculty or staff is irreparably below necessary standards, it is both expedient and humane to terminate that person's employment at the earliest opportunity that is contractually possible.

An example of violating unwritten rule #1 occurs when search committees decide to grant courtesy interviews to candidates who have no realistic chance of being hired or to allow the application of an unsuitable candidate for a grant, award, or other opportunity to remain until late in the process "to give the person some experience." When those who apply for opportunities are not screened out throughout successive phases of the review, they become more and more confident that they'll ultimately be successful. That same experience can be found in the faculty evaluation process. For instance, a faculty member who goes through six or seven years of probation, only to be denied tenure and promotion at the end, is likely to feel much more unfairly treated than someone whose contract is not renewed after only two or three years. The latter person will often feel that the situation just didn't work out or that he or she wasn't a good fit for the institution, whereas the longer-term employee may feel strung along, taken advantage of, and misled.

Probationary review committees occasionally feel that the most generous option is to provide the faculty member with employment as long as possible because a termination decision doesn't have to be made yet. But that approach misrepresents the actual situation for the faculty member and has the potential for causing the institution great problems in the future. After all, if the faculty member is not renewed three or four years in the future, the question is likely to be asked, "What changed since the time of the probationary pretenure review?" And the answer might be that nothing has actually changed, but rather a pattern of unsatisfactory performance had been observed earlier, even though it hadn't been acted on. It's precisely that type of thinking that gets administrators and committees into trouble.

In most cases, if the review committee's decision truly is that the faculty member is highly unlikely to be approved for tenure, promotion, or a multiyear contract in the future, the best and most compassionate choice is usually to recommend that, at the earliest possible opportunity, the faculty member's contract not be renewed. If it still seems desirable to offer continued probationary employment even though a long-term contract will almost certainly not be offered, it's incumbent on the reviewer to make a compelling case for why such an offer should be made. Keep in mind that you may well have to answer for this decision not merely now but also if the matter proceeds to a grievance or lawsuit several years in the future.

○ considerations resulting from the formative nature of probationary reviews

Fortunately, in only a minority of situations will a probationary review result in the termination of the faculty member. It's far more common for the conclusion to be either that the faculty member is doing precisely the right things to receive a positive decision in the future or that challenges do exist but can be overcome. In these common situations, the entire focus of the probationary period pretenure review can be formative. You will therefore need to ask those questions that we saw earlier.

If the faculty member is making adequate progress, what advice can be given so as to increase his or her likelihood of success even more?

We might refer to this situation as the "frosting on the cake" scenario. In other words, even if the faculty does nothing more than continue to teach at the quality that has already been documented, produce research at the rate that has occurred during the past several years, and continue engaging in a similar number of service activities, a positive decision for tenure, promotion, or an extended contract seems probable. Many review committees are content to say, "Keep up the good work!" and proceed to the next candidate, but there is also an opportunity to demonstrate some excellent mentoring here. If the foundation that the faculty member has prepared is so strong, are there appropriate ways in which expectations can be increased even further for the future? Is there evidence in the application that the person has the potential of becoming a faculty leader and should be encouraged to take on greater responsibilities? It can be beneficial to encourage the review committee to look beyond its current task and see whether any of the following opportunities may be appropriate for the faculty member who clearly has met and then exceeded expectations for the probationary review:

- Undergoing a final review for tenure, promotion, or a multiple-year contract ahead of the usual schedule
- Being considered for an institutional, regional, or national award for excellence in teaching
- Raising the bar in research activity by seeking larger and more competitive grants, publications by more selective journals or presses, prizes and fellowships for creative work, and the like
- Service on more prominent committees such as those that consider curricular proposals for the institution as a whole, screen and interview candidates for major administrative positions, engage in faculty governance, or assume similar responsibilities that extend far beyond the discipline
- Seeking national or international office in a disciplinary organization or taking the initial steps that could eventually lead to such an office
- Receiving training in academic leadership that will better prepare the faculty member for future positions such as department chair, dean, or provost

When seen from these perspectives, the issues become less about recommending desired improvements than about expanding the range of the faculty member's possibilities. For one thing, the recommendations you make can help transform a future tenure application from a very strong case into a forgone conclusion. For another, it's clear from the committee's review that the faculty member is someone with a great deal of potential, and both the discipline and the entire institution will be best served by directing that potential to the most meaningful goals.

If you decide to pursue this strategy, make it clear to the person you're reviewing that you're not raising the bar because you feel the faculty member needs to improve, but that your recommendations are a vote of confidence in his or her ability to accomplish even greater things.

If the faculty member's application demonstrates areas of weaknesses that can be improved before the final tenure review, what recommendations should be given so as to make a positive evaluation more likely?
In Chapter Three, we saw how unhelpful it can be to make overly general or overly explicit observations. Constructive criticism should always give a clear idea of the level of achievement that the reviewer was anticipating and why that level of achievement is significant, but it shouldn't be so prescriptive that the faculty member has no opportunities for innovation and creativity. For this reason, a more helpful way in which to begin giving advice is the following:

> Since we define ourselves as a research university, and even our instructional mission involves teaching students how to engage in original scholarship, it's important for us to demonstrate in every tenure application that a faculty member has clearly demonstrated his or her ability to conduct significant research within the context of our facilities, equipment, and teaching load.
>
> In your first three years of full-time work, you did produce one excellent article that appeared in a top-rated journal. But when you come up for tenure in three years, the expectation will be that you will have produced approximately one such article each year and received funding for at least one external grant proposal greater than $250,000. So based on what we're seeing so far, you're not yet on track for a positive tenure recommendation.

In this hypothetical case, it may have been the fact that the single article that was produced appeared in a highly rated journal that made the committee believe that adequate progress was still possible. The next stage, therefore, is to give clear guidance as to what that adequate progress would entail. This advice should be expressed in such a manner that it will be clear to an impartial observer whether the advice has been followed and the recommended goals achieved:

> For this reason, we're going to review your portfolio again in one year. Within the next ten weeks, you should draw up a work plan indicating how you intend to meet the goal of roughly one refereed article per year—or six in all by the time of your tenure review—and one successfully funded external grant of at least $250,000. You've already demonstrated your capacity to publish in a top-tier journal, so we're going to work with you to develop a list of acceptable journals in which your research can be published, including several that have slightly higher rates of acceptance.

In this way, rather than offering vague advice to "do better in the future," the committee is offering a well-defined plan with specific goals, a time line, and a discussion of standards. As a matter of effective management, it may be useful to follow this advice with a statement that although these objectives will be hard to meet and ultimate success is still uncertain, the reviewers are making this recommendation because they're confident that the faculty member is capable of achieving these challenging results. After all, if the consensus had been that the faculty member was extremely unlikely to receive tenure, you probably wouldn't make recommendations about specific courses of action. So it's usually beneficial to combine encouragement with a frank assessment of the challenges that need to be addressed.

The primary goal is to avoid giving the faculty member mixed messages. In general, matters may look generally good now, but no one can promise that the result will inevitably be positive a few years down the road. Or challenges may exist now, but it would be counterproductive to be so negative that the faculty member gives up hope when all that was needed is a slight adjustment or a bit of training.

Providing this type of specific, constructive, and forward-looking advice is advantageous no matter what the faculty member's particular weakness may be. Here are a few examples of phrasing that can be used to deal with various deficiencies in a candidate's application:

Although it's clear that you put a great deal of care and effort into your course preparations, it's also clear that the results—based on our review of student course evaluations, the reports of your peers, and the record of your students in subsequent courses—aren't commensurate with your exertions. We have concluded, therefore, that you should attend at least six workshops on active learning and alternative classroom techniques offered by our Center for Excellence in Teaching and Learning. We will also schedule regular meetings for you with a faculty mentor in an appropriate discipline who has received the university's medal for Excellence in Undergraduate Instruction. Then that faculty mentor and someone in a related discipline who works in our Master Teacher Program will observe your classes and report to me as your supervisor whether they believe your quality of instruction has improved. We'll also be checking the results of future student course evaluations and the record of the students in your courses this semester as they advance to subsequent courses.

One area that did cause concern for the reviewers is your level of contributions to service. The two committees of which you have been a member certainly provide important service, but none of your activities appears to have had much of an impact on the college, university, or community as a whole. We strongly urge you to meet annually for the next three years with your chair and the head of the Promotion and Tenure Committee in order to identify service activities that are most likely to strengthen your portfolio for the future. Moreover, since our institutional guidelines state that community service learning projects may be counted as credit for either teaching or service, we recommend that you move those accomplishments from the teaching section of your application (which is sufficiently strong without them) to the service section (which appears quite brief by comparison).

Despite this strong record in teaching, research, and scholarship, the committee notes that you may find it extremely difficult to receive a positive recommendation for tenure from your department unless you address certain issues related to collegiality. In their reports to the committee, significantly more than half of your peers noted that behaviors such as excessive irritability, frequent displays of anger, and public humiliation of others were hampering their professional activities by making faculty members avoid department meetings (resulting in the lack of a quorum) or prolonging discussions far beyond the point that most members found constructive. We encourage you to refrain from these behaviors, starting immediately, and to request aid from the employee assistance program or university counseling center if you believe that these behaviors are beyond your individual control.

○ dealing with hostility or denial during a probationary review

Even the best preparation for a faculty evaluation and the most careful phrasing used in conveying the result can never guarantee that the results will be received with appreciation and full acceptance. It's in human nature to find criticism unpleasant, and certain people will not be pleased with any result other than effusive praise. Although hostile reactions tend to be far more intense when criticism is conveyed during promotion or tenure reviews (since the stakes are so high) or after a posttenure review (since highly experienced faculty members often believe that they alone know best about how to succeed in their courses and research), it's not at all uncommon for someone to react to a negative probationary review with belligerence, resistance, or denial. In these cases, there are several options you might wish to consider:

○ *If the result of the review is so negative that there is a recommendation not to renew the faculty member's contract, direct the faculty member to the office of human resources or the university counsel, not the department or review committee.* Almost every system of probationary review has at least some appeal process. The faculty member's first recourse if he or she objects to the result of a review is to follow the established procedure for having the decision reconsidered. One complexity that may arise is that since the faculty member is not yet entitled to an expectation of continued employment, each year's contract technically entails a self-contained period of employment. In other words, unless your institutional policy dictates otherwise, you are technically under no obligation to give the faculty member any reason whatsoever for the nonrenewal. As a result, most appeals to probationary reviews involve only a consideration of whether the correct procedure was followed, not whether the result was justified. For this reason, since any objection that the faculty member now has must involve a contractual and procedural issue rather than the internal discussions of the review committee, these concerns are better handled by the office of human resources or the university counsel, not you. You'd be well advised to deflect any further inquiries or statements from the faculty member to those offices and avoid complicating the matter by responding in a way that may cause further problems later. And in your own case, always make sure to consult with legal counsel and the office of human resources before delivering news of nonrenewal of a faculty member's contract.

○ *Remind the faculty member that probationary reviews are the efforts of his or her colleagues to provide helpful advice.* If the recommendation doesn't involve nonrenewal but recommends improvements over the next two to three years, your best approach to a hostile faculty member will be different. In these cases, it's frequently useful to remind the faculty member what a probationary review actually is: an effort by his or her peers to be helpful in noting ways in which this application can be strengthened when it's ultimately considered for tenure, promotion, or a multiyear contract. The faculty member is free to accept the advice or reject it, but ignoring these recommendations is probably at the applicant's peril. To begin with, he or she has to remember that the reviewers gave freely of their time and effort in order to be as helpful as possible. Second, since it's likely that the review committee for the more substantive evaluation scheduled to occur in a few years will contain some of the same members as the current committee, it seems politically unwise to reject these suggestions outright. Part of what the future committee may do is to examine how well the recommendations of the probationary review committee have been followed. So even if the faculty member does not agree with the suggestions that have been made, it's probably imprudent to ignore them entirely.

o *In the case of denial, review with the faculty member what the committee's specific concerns were and how they may best be addressed.* Sometimes a faculty member's reaction to criticism during a probationary review isn't hostility about the result but denial that the recommendations relate to actual problems. In these cases, it can be useful to express confidence in the faculty member's ability to address these concerns before subsequent evaluations occur and to consider whether the committee was responding to a lack of sufficient progress or adequate documentation. If the faculty member truly believes that the expected standards of achievement had been fully met but that "the committee simply didn't see it," shift your focus from improving the person's performance to improving his or her application. Recommend a few ways in which the faculty member can make the job of the review committee easier by organizing materials in a more effective manner, expanding the type of documentation that's provided, or tying the materials submitted more closely to the standards by which they'll be reviewed. Provide constructive advice on ways in which he or she can make a stronger case rather than suggest that such a case could not have been made at all based on the faculty member's level of performance.

mini-case studies: probationary period pretenure reviews

You're chairing a review committee that's conducting a three-year review of a probationary tenure-track faculty member. Reaching consensus is difficult because the candidate you're reviewing has an inconsistent record, with certain excellent achievements punctuating periods of mediocre or even poor performance. Half the members of your committee think that the best solution is to cut your losses now and recommend that the contract not be renewed.

(Continued)

Their argument is that the goal of a probationary review is to determine whether adequate progress is being made toward tenure, and the faculty member's application suggests that a strong case can't be made. "If the decision is difficult now," they say, "it'll be all the more difficult in three years when we do a tenure evaluation. If we recommend denial now, at least this person won't have a failed tenure application to justify when applying for other jobs. The most humane and responsible decision is to let this person go and see if we can be more successful with the next hire." The other half of the committee feels that when the decision could go either way, the benefit of the doubt should always go to the faculty member. "The whole purpose of a three-year review," this side argues, "is to recommend what a tenure-track faculty member needs to do in order to earn tenure. There's nothing in this application that's bad enough to warrant an outright dismissal. We have a moral and professional obligation to state what has to be done during the next three years to make this faculty member's application suitable for a positive tenure vote. After we make our recommendation, it's up to the applicant either to follow through on our recommendations or not. But our job is to provide constructive advice."

Despite heated discussions, the members of the committee are evenly split on what to recommend, and so the deciding vote is yours. What do you do, and why?

o . o   o

You've participated in a probationary review of a faculty member that resulted in a positive recommendation for continuation of annual contracts but also raised some serious issues that the committee felt needed to be addressed. Several days after announcing this decision, you are met by the faculty member in your office. The faculty member has concerns because several of the issues that the review committee has raised seem to fall into a gray area between the personal freedoms the university has pledged to protect and the professional standards it's committed to uphold. One of the committee's conclusions, for example, was that the faculty member was highly ineffective in teaching because of poor communication skills. Student course evaluations frequently note that the professor is extremely difficult to understand in class, an observation verified through numerous peer reports. Since the faculty member is not a native citizen and learned English only late in life, you're getting ready to summarize the efforts that the institution can make in order to help employees reduce their accents and improve their use of grammar, but then the faculty member interrupts you. "That's not the issue," the faculty member says and notes that what makes it difficult for students to understand what is said in the classroom is the nature of head covering that the professor's religion requires all adult members to wear. "I cannot be clearly understood without violating the dictates of my religion, an interference forbidden by this school's own nondiscrimination policy, and I cannot meet the requirement your committee has imposed without improving my ability to be understood."

You are digesting this new piece of information when you learn that there's more: "In addition, the traditions of my country of origin, as well as my religion, forbid me from condoning or having contact with individuals who engage in 'deviant' sexual practices. Every single qualified graduate student who can work with me on my research team is either homosexual or transgendered, and I am utterly unable to work with them. That is why my research agenda has fallen so far behind. But you can't enforce their equal opportunity rights without violating mine, and if I am ultimately denied tenure on this issue, it will certainly result in a major lawsuit and unfavorable publicity for this institution, as well as you personally."

How do you handle this situation? What other campus offices should become involved in addressing the issue? Although it would have been far better for this issue to have been addressed long before, since that didn't occur, what's the best course of action to take now?

o o o

At the urging of the faculty senate, your institution has adopted a new policy that allocates special development funding for faculty members who pass a probationary pretenure review but are found to have specific deficiencies in either teaching or research. The response to this initiative has been far greater than anyone had predicted, and so the institution has been unable to provide funding for every individual who qualifies under the guidelines. This year, the area you supervise has two faculty members who underwent third-year reviews. Both passed the review, although both also received a number of recommendations for improvement. In addition, the committee responsible for allocating the special development funding (and you are not a member of this committee) decided to provide an improvement grant to one of these faculty members, even though it couldn't address the needs of both.

(Continued)

Faculty member A, who received the grant, had significant deficiencies in teaching effectiveness, and the funding is intended to support attendance at a workshop that addresses the specific problem this faculty member is having. Faculty member B, while having several key weaknesses, had an overall stronger application than faculty member A, so the committee felt that with funding being limited, faculty member B was more likely to receive tenure unaided than was faculty member A. Nevertheless, from a reference call you received, you know that faculty member A is already planning to accept a position at a rival institution but hasn't yet made a public announcement because he or she wants access to this special development funding before leaving. The colleague who called you for a recommendation of faculty member A asked (but could not require) that you be discreet, and you promised to abide by that request. But all of that occurred before you knew about faculty member A's plans to spend the development funding before resigning. Since you're going to lose faculty member A in any case and since faculty member B could benefit from the special funding, do you break your promise of confidence and tell your supervisor or the committee about what faculty member A intends to do?

o conclusion

Although some pretenure reviews are summative in that they lead to nonrenewal of the faculty member's contract, probationary reviews in the vast majority of cases have a primarily formative purpose. And while many institutions regard the probationary period pretenure review as a less formal or intensive evaluation than those conducted for tenure, promotion, or posttenure review, the impact this process can have both on the institution and the faculty member means that it should be approached with great seriousness and care. In the case of someone who isn't working out, for whatever reason, and is thus unlikely to succeed in future evaluations, the summative aspect of probationary evaluations offers the possibility of not renewing the person's contract at an early date. Nevertheless, the formative aspect of most probationary reviews allows faculty members to assist one another in a collegial manner to improve the performance of one of their peers, encourage his or her further development, and increase the likelihood of a successful outcome in later processes.

References

Diamond, R. M. (2004). *Preparing for promotion, tenure, and annual review: A faculty guide* (2nd ed.). San Francisco: Jossey-Bass/Anker.

Resources

Drum, C., Seale, C., & Crump, M. (2008). Establishing a pretenure review program in an academic library. *Library Administration and Management, 22*(1), 31–36.

Fuss, D. (2007). The junior faculty handbook. *Profession, 2007*(1), 107–115.

Ortlieb, E. T., Biddix, J. P., & Doepker, G. M. (2010). A collaborative approach to higher education induction. *Active Learning in Higher Education, 11*(2), 109–118.

6

posttenure review

Posttenure review originated as a result of the same drive toward greater accountability in higher education that we explored in Chapter One, although somewhat later than the other processes we've examined (Licata and Morreale, 1999). Certain legislatures, governing boards, and universities felt there was a need to ensure that faculty productivity didn't taper off once an individual was tenured. As an effort to weed out "deadwood," posttenure review was given added impetus in 1986 when American universities could no longer enforce mandatory retirement ages, thus being left with relatively few mechanisms for ridding themselves of tenured poor performers.

Despite the largely negative nature of this original focus, the outcome of posttenure review as it's actually practiced seems much more likely to entail confirmation that the faculty member under evaluation is still meeting or exceeding the institution's standards for performance or, at worst, in need of some collegial advice about how to become more effective. While certain faculty members may well choose to retire rather than undergo a posttenure review process that's likely to result in criticism, it's relatively uncommon for tenured professors to be terminated as the result of a single posttenure review. For this reason, posttenure review is rather similar to a probationary pretenure review: while acting as a summative process in a minority of cases, for most faculty members it's formative in nature and serves to improve performance rather than punish failure.

The mere threat that posttenure review could cause a weakening of the tenure system in the United States has caused this process to be eyed warily by such organizations as the American Association of University Professors (1999):

> The Association believes that periodic formal institutional evaluation of each postprobationary faculty member would bring scant benefit, would incur unacceptable costs, not only in money and time but also in dampening of creativity and of collegial relationships, and would threaten academic freedom. The Association emphasizes that no procedure for evaluation of faculty should be used to weaken or undermine the principles of academic freedom and tenure. The Association cautions particularly against allowing any general system of evaluation to be used as grounds for dismissal or other disciplinary sanctions.

Despite these cautions, Peter Seldin (1999) has detected "a noticeable trend in public institutions and systems to attempt to build sanctions into . . . post-tenure review programs," including dismissal for a repeated pattern of ineffective teaching (pp. 133–134). In addition, a study conducted by Kerry Ann O'Meara (2004) confirmed that many faculty members believe that posttenure review destroys the fundamental principles behind tenure, reduces their autonomy, and requires redundant work.

Professors' buy-in to the process of posttenure review is thus often less when they're required to submit materials for posttenure review than when they undergo evaluation for tenure, promotion, and merit increases. In the latter cases, most people believe that they're documenting their achievements in a way that could well be to their benefit. In the case of posttenure review, they often feel that they are engaging in a great deal of effort for a process that at best leaves them exactly where they are currently and, at worst, could end their careers. In addition, posttenure review is almost always a newer (and less familiar) process than other types of evaluation and thus tends to produce the anxiety of the unfamiliar.

Is there any way for deans, department chairs, and committee members who are required to conduct posttenure reviews to ensure that this process achieves its goal of encouraging continual development of the senior faculty without undermining "the principles of academic freedom and tenure"? How, in other words, can reviewers help post-tenure review do the things that it should do while working within a system that prescribes what they must do?

○ preserving a constructive and future-oriented approach toward posttenure review

The system that your institution has established for posttenure review will circumscribe your options in conducting the evaluation and report-ing the results. But within these restrictions, it's to your advantage to make that entire process as constructive and future oriented as possible.

Let's imagine a university where there are only two possible results of posttenure review: the faculty member is judged to be performing at either a satisfactory or an unsatisfactory level. It can be a blow to morale for a highly accomplished senior faculty member to spend weeks assem-bling the information required for the evaluation when the best result that can be expected is to be declared no better than "satisfactory." So unless forbidden by institutional policy, it can make all the difference in the world for the chair of the review committee (or perhaps the com-mittee as a whole) to conduct a follow-up meeting with the faculty member and say something like the following:

> Even though the procedure says that each faculty member has to be rated either satisfactory or unsatisfactory, we wanted you to know how far beyond the mere requirements your performance has been. In addition to having been a model teacher, you've clearly been a mentor to your students and have been instrumental to their success

for many years. Your research has brought positive attention, not just to your own discipline, but to the institution as a whole. And your level of service has made you the type of academic citizen that we all aspire to be. For this reason, even though we were limited in terms of what the result of this process could be, we wanted you to know how inspirational we ourselves found the materials that you submitted and how fortunate we are to be your colleagues.

A statement of this sort can help make the onerous task of gathering and preparing documentation seem a bit more worthwhile. In a similar way, when less positive news has to be conveyed, it can be provided in a context that places less emphasis on the mistakes of the past than on the possibilities for the future:

> We know that anyone's first reaction to seeing a result like "unsatisfactory" is likely to be disappointment, offense, and even anger. But it's important to recognize that what this evaluation really means is that we, as your colleagues, feel that the last few years have not been as reflective of the high quality of work we know you're capable of and for which you were awarded tenure in the first place. And we have some suggestions that we think can help to bring your record and your obvious abilities more into line. What we'd like to suggest is . . .

Conversations like these help keep the faculty member's focus on the positive, future-oriented aspects of the review and can make a significant difference in the degree of support people have for the process. Moreover, there are several other sound evaluation procedures that Christine Licata and Joseph Morreale (1999) have found to be present in the most successful posttenure review procedures:

• As in any other type of faculty review, the criteria and standards on which the evaluation is based must be well understood by all participants. It's impossible for the faculty member being reviewed to prepare an appropriate dossier unless he or she knows in advance what the review committee will be looking for, how they will be making their decisions, and what type of documentation they are expecting. Similarly, anyone who reviews these materials must have a clear understanding of what is and is not relevant to the type of evaluation being conducted. If the same standards that are used for tenure or promotion decisions remain applicable, then this requirement should be explicitly stated. If a certain level of growth and development after the individual's last major personnel decision is expected, there should be an indication of how much additional achievement is deemed appropriate. If departments or local units are free to set their own standards or to use those in place for the regular annual evaluation, then that too should be specified. In short, since there is no one universally accepted set of standards and criteria for posttenure review worldwide, it'll be easy for the review committee, as well as the faculty member being evaluated, to make incorrect assumptions about those standards unless they're clarified in advance.

- Multiple sources of information, including those that may not be available to the faculty member under review, should be considered. A posttenure review that simply examines a faculty member's curriculum vitae is unlikely to have much value. There are too many dimensions to faculty work to draw meaningful conclusions from a résumé alone. In a similar way, student course evaluations can be a valuable source of information about quality of instruction, but as we saw in Chapter Two, they don't reveal everything a committee needs to know about a faculty member's teaching. For this reason, follow your institution's guidelines, but whenever possible, consult as many sources of information as those guidelines allow. Letters from former students, peers, administrators, and external reviewers can be revealing. The extent to which a faculty member's articles are cited by others, as indicated by such metrics as the Eigenfactor, the Impact Factor of the ISI (Institute for Scientific Information), or Scopus's Source Normalized Impact per Paper, provides an indication of how much influence a faculty member's research has had on other scholars. Reports from committee chairs about the degree to which a faculty member participated constructively in meetings are a lot more informative than a list of committees alone. In general, try to ask, "What is it that we really need to know in order to draw our conclusions, and what are the best, most objective sources of that information?"

- The process includes an opportunity for the faculty member to engage in a reflective self-evaluation. Our own perceptions of how well we perform are not always the same as how others see our work. We may think we're achieving spectacular results, but our colleagues may have serious concerns about the quality of our contributions, or we might be overly concerned about disappointments and "failures" even though others regard us as a star performer. Self-evaluations allow posttenure review committees to determine whether the faculty member is being realistic about his or her own strengths, weaknesses, achievements, and goals. No matter whether the overall result of the evaluation is positive or negative, this self-appraisal will be useful in forming a professional development plan for the future and in discussing new directions the faculty member believes are desirable and important.

- The advice that is provided should be constructive in nature and incorporate a focus on career growth and appropriate objectives for professional development. Licata and Morreale (1999) note that best practices in posttenure review involve assisting the faculty member with planning for activities not merely in the immediate future or until the time of the next posttenure review, but throughout the rest of his or her career. It may well be that the faculty member's discipline (or personal situation) is changing so significantly that serious long-term planning is required. That type of career planning is not something that one does only at the start of one's professional life but also every three to five years thereafter. Formal posttenure review processes offer convenient points at which to encourage a serious discussion of a faculty member's options and strategies in the period ahead.

- The process should be equally meaningful for star performers, those with solid records of achievement, and those in need of improvement. Despite the reasons for its origination, posttenure review is least effective when it's conducted as a punitive process design to weed out deadwood (and hence waste the time of everyone else). Rather, it should contain mechanisms for rewarding those whose work has been stellar, provide constructive advice to those who are doing well but could do even better, and advise or make other appropriate decisions about faculty members whose performance has declined substantially since the granting of tenure.

There are also two other recommendations for conducting effective posttenure reviews that William Plater (2001) discusses on making this process as positive and constructive as possible:

○ *The dialogue about posttenure review should include everyone affected by tenure.* Although institutions may decide that posttenure review committees should consist of only those who are already tenured (or perhaps even tenured full professors), there are compelling reasons for including junior faculty members in the process at least to some degree. Less experienced instructors are the very individuals the college or university wants to remain as professionally active and engaged as possible throughout their entire careers. It thus makes good sense for them to understand the expectations that lie ahead. Just as a grading rubric is less effective when it's shared with students only after their grades have been assigned, so are the advantages of posttenure review lost if people have direct exposure to its standards and criteria only when they must prepare their own portfolios. Including tenure-track faculty members in initial discussions about the process, when the purpose, timetable, and desired benchmarks are discussed, alerts them to what they'll need to accomplish in the future and, in this way, plays an important developmental role.

o   *Peer evaluation is the foundation of effective posttenure review.*
Regardless of how many sources are consulted for information
about a faculty member's performance, it is ultimately peers—not
the supervisor alone, student course evaluations alone, or any other
single set of data—who should decide whether someone's overall
performance has remained at a high level and, if not, what needs to
be addressed. Colleagues in the person's discipline are best positioned to determine whether appropriate standards of performance
have been reached in light of current teaching loads, expectations
for research, and obligations for service:

> Those institutions that are most likely to implement post-tenure
> review successfully will rely on the judgment of peers to give credibil-
> ity and legitimacy both to the act of assessing faculty performance
> and to individual judgments. While many faculty flinch at the idea of
> criticizing colleagues with whom they have the long-term relationship
> that tenure creates, one of the responsibilities of tenure is to engage
> genuinely with one's peers through the kind of tough-minded
> feedback that characterizes both vibrant scholarship and effective
> post-tenure reviews [Plater, 2001, p. 56].

Finally, it might be beneficial to add one final best practice that I
have found to be important: Posttenure reviews should have the ability
to recognize and reward star performers, not merely address the problems of underachievers. As we've already seen, the most effective posttenure review systems, and the ones that develop the strongest faculty
buy-in, tend to be those that have the flexibility to reward people for
stellar work in addition to providing corrective action for unsatisfactory
work. For instance, at Georgia Southern University, the policy on posttenure review states that the purpose of this activity is "to recognize,
reward, and enhance the performance of tenured faculty . . . to recognize and reward tenured faculty who have made and continue to make
significant contributions to the missions of their departments, colleges,
and the University" (http://academics.georgiasouthern.edu/provost/
handbook/section200_1_13). These recognitions and rewards can

include bonuses, additional merit increases, and other highly desirable types of compensation.

Similarly, Texas Tech University has a number of innovative strategies to reward faculty members for a highly positive posttenure review (personal communication with Bob Smith, provost of Texas Tech University, August 8, 2011; see also Seldin, 1999):

- The chancellor confers two separate awards with a cash prize of five thousand dollars each year for outstanding teaching and research.
- The president presents an award of fifteen hundred dollars plus a university medallion to a faculty member in every college each year in recognition of outstanding teaching.
- As many as three President's Academic Achievement awards of two thousand dollars plus a university medallion are made every year to faculty members who have outstanding records in teaching, research, and service.
- The provost identifies twelve faculty members each year as Integrated Scholars—professors who are not only outstanding in teaching, research, and service but also find innovative ways to blend these three elements—with a number of special distinctions attached.
- The university recognizes its foremost faculty members as Horn Professors, a distinction that comes with a permanent salary increase of eight thousand dollars and an allocation of twenty thousand dollars each year that may be used to support the faculty member's scholarship and research.

○ benefiting from best practices regardless of your current procedures

The question then arises, "How can I make use of all these wonderful ideas if certain elements of them—such as self-evaluations, extensive peer reviews, and rewards for superior performance—aren't part of the system my institution uses?" An effective way to answer this question is to adopt a twofold strategy. First, since these best practices have clear advantages for both the faculty member and institution, work within your school's policies to see that more of these practices are incorporated into your procedure. Second, try to apply the benefits of these ideas into your existing process in ways that don't violate any policies already in place. For example, if your institution doesn't provide any mechanism for rewarding and recognizing outstanding performers during posttenure, explore ways in which you can remedy this oversight at the department or college level. Allocate an increase in travel or research funding, if that's possible, to those whose results surpass a certain standard or acknowledge the person's achievement in a public manner. Start the tradition of a multiplate plaque on which the names of posttenure review stars can be acknowledged for posterity. If none of these alternatives will work at your institution, host a dinner or lunch in the person's honor.

Even if your system doesn't formally establish a procedure for gathering insights from peers, students, and other stakeholders in the faculty member's performance, make it clear that you as a reviewer need these sources of information in order to conduct a fair and thorough evaluation. Gather insights informally that other universities collect more formally and thus broaden the scope of the perspectives that you consider. It's very rare that these best practices are strictly forbidden by an institution's policy (and you should work to change that policy if this is the case). It's more common that these practices haven't been considered. As a reviewer, you'll want to do everything you can in order to make the review impartial, comprehensive, and forward looking. The sound evaluation procedures outlined above are excellent ways of moving toward this goal.

Conducting Regular Reviews Versus Triggered Reviews

Posttenure review systems generally fall into two categories: those that evaluate every tenured faculty member periodically and those that are triggered by some occurrence, such as low student or peer evaluations, the request of a chair, or multiple years of substandard performance on annual evaluations. Some institutions prefer the latter type of review because it proves less onerous and costly. They may argue, "Why should we waste people's time when we know they're doing well? Why should we force faculty members with excellent records to jump through this unnecessary hoop?" The fact is, however, that universal posttenure reviews are preferable to targeted ones for several reasons.

First, it's not the case that excellent faculty members can't do even better. The people who have the most accomplished records in teaching, research, and service are often those who value additional advice on how to keep on improving. Second, if your evaluation system or your own personal practice permits rewarding star performers, then excusing good faculty members from this process deprives you of an opportunity to congratulate them on their superior work, recognize their achievements, and hold them up as models for others to emulate. Third, and most important, triggered posttenure review processes create an environment in which morale is likely to plummet and the number of appeals or grievances is likely to rise. Many people at your institution will view requiring only those for whom there are problems to undergo an extensive review process as akin to declaring someone a criminal before the trial even begins. It will be well known that the only people who have to go up for review are those for whom "there are issues." Afterward, students and faculty members may recall only this negative impression even if the result of the evaluation was positively glowing.

For all these reasons, it's highly desirable to advocate for a system in which every tenured faculty member—perhaps annually, perhaps every three to five years—submits a portfolio of materials and receives the constructive criticism of his or her peers. Once this process is built into your system, it's not particularly difficult for faculty members to retain the items they submitted for their tenure or promotion reviews, update them as necessary, and allow them to be examined by the appropriate reviewers.

As we've seen, certain types of information, such as the results of student course evaluations and the comparison of the faculty member's own rating to those of others in the discipline and at the institution, don't even have to be prepared by the person undergoing review. These metrics are better calculated centrally in order to provide the highest degree of consistency and accuracy. Although there may well be initial resistance to the requirement that faculty members gather yet another set of documents for what they may view as "yet another pointless administrative procedure," these objections will diminish once people begin to see the value of the process, including any rewards and recognition they may gain from it. And their resistance will certainly be far less if they understand that everyone is being asked to engage in this process, not merely those for whom the administration has concerns.

Handling the Negative Results of a Posttenure Review

Any type of evaluation that leads to a negative result could result in a faculty member who's angry or depressed, ready to file a grievance, prepared to take legal action, and convinced that the reviewers don't know what they're doing. These reactions tend to be most pronounced after tenure evaluations, because the stakes are so high, and after posttenure reviews, because faculty members with a great deal of experience may be shocked to learn that they're not universally regarded as well above average.

As we saw in the case of nonrenewal decisions in Chapter Five, there is great value in having objections, appeals, and concerns about any result that could lead to termination handled elsewhere at the institution (that is, not in your own office). In the case of posttenure reviews, it's probably best to direct all complaints to one level above where the review was conducted. In other words, if your institutional policy states that posttenure review should be conducted at the departmental level, direct any objections to the dean. If this process is conducted at the dean's level, direct them to the provost, and so on. The supervising office will be in the best possible position to verify that appropriate procedures were followed and that all of the relevant information was duly considered.

If the decision has been so strongly negative that the recommendation is for tenure to be revoked and the procedure for termination to be implemented, then complaints and appeals should be directed to the office of human resources or the university counsel. If you've adhered to the advice recommended in Chapter Two to follow your institution's established procedures to the letter and kept good records, you'll have done what's necessary to permit those offices to verify that the decision was fair, impartially reached, and appropriate.

Even with the assistance of other offices in supporting you after having made a negative decision, dealing with the faculty member's response can be uncomfortable, and sometimes even frightening. The following precautions are advisable for any such situation where you find yourself uneasy:

- If you have any reason at all to feel that your safety or that of other committee members may be in jeopardy, don't hesitate to alert the institution's security office or police force.
- Refuse to allow yourself to be blindsided by the person's anger and distress. If the faculty member tries to engage you in a conversation when you're not prepared for it, insist that the discussion be scheduled, and have an appropriate third party (your supervisor, a university attorney, or a member of the human resources staff) present at that time.
- Make it clear that the decision wasn't a personal attack on the faculty member or a rejection of him or her as a person, even though it may feel that way at the time. Repeat as often as necessary that your job was to apply the institution's policy and criteria to the portfolio in accordance with your best professional judgment, and that's precisely what you have done.
- Avoid statements containing the words *you* and *your* as much as possible. For example, rather than saying, "The standards that are in place wouldn't permit us to pass you because of your scholarship," say "The amount [or "the level"] of the scholarship that was documented did not meet existing standards." Second-person forms often feel demeaning or accusatory, even when they're not intended that way.

- Don't tell the person to calm down. Statements of this sort often exacerbate the person's frustration and anger. Instead, say something like, "I fully understand how you feel. I'd feel exactly the same way in this situation. But I assure you that we [I] followed every one of the guidelines in place, and this decision was the only one that could be made in those circumstances."
- Don't allow the person to use the tactic of, "But I thought we were friends." Reiterate that this decision had to be one of professional judgment; personal feelings didn't come into play.
- Let the person vent if that's what he or she needs and you're in a situation where that's appropriate. Sometimes people in disappointing situations have to direct their feelings toward someone, and since you're a visible symbol of what has caused his or her distress, you may simply be a convenient target. If your safety isn't threatened, you have the time, and there are no inappropriate parties (such as students or potential donors) present, the person may feel better simply by expressing to you how he or she is feeling.
- Don't be tricked into apologizing. A well-intentioned desire to make an unhappy person feel better can sometimes lead people to apologize even when the problem isn't their fault. In the case of responses to negative evaluation decisions, that type of pro forma apology is dangerous. It can increase the other person's anger toward you and be regarded as an admission of culpability should the matter come to a grievance or lawsuit.
- Don't anticipate that you'll be able to reason the person out of his or her anger. At the moment, reason has very little to do with how he or she feels, and if you expect that logic is going to resolve the situation, you'll be in for a bitter disappointment.
- Don't respond with anger or frustration yourself. Even if the person's behavior irritates you severely, responding in kind will merely throw fuel on a blazing fire. In addition, you're more likely to say something that you'll regret later.
- Don't be patronizing. This person is experiencing a severe blow to his or her career, ego, and possibly income. These are serious

matters. It's much better to be supportive and compassionate at such a time than to make the person feel like a failure.

- Find something the two of you can agree on. Having a shared focus reestablishes rapport and reminds the person that you aren't really the enemy. Say something like, "In terms of teaching and service, your work has been exceptional. I was really impressed reading your portfolio, and I know you have to be proud too of what your former students say about you."
- Don't interrupt to correct minor details. If the person says, "Now, that memo you wrote me last Thursday . . . ," saying, "It was Friday," adds nothing of value to the conversation and may well cause the other person's anger to escalate.
- After the encounter is over, write yourself a brief summary of what occurred so that it's documented in case of future inquiries.

Keep in mind as you adopt these strategies for responding to what the faculty member is thinking that these approaches shouldn't be used formulaically, as though you're using a management tool to "deal with" that person. If the faculty member feels that he or she is being manipulated, your actions will have made the situation worse, not better.

mini-case studies: probationary posttenure reviews

You head your institution's posttenure review committee, and the other members have presented you with a challenge. One of your faculty members, Dr. Jekyll, has had a career that began with a highly impressive level of performance but hasn't been successful more recently. After winning a major international prize for research while only an assistant professor, Dr. Jekyll over the next few years won every teaching award imaginable, published in first-tier journals, and sailed through evaluations for promotion and tenure. But then something seemed to go wrong. Teaching evaluations from students and peers went from spectacular to good to poor to terrible, research

(Continued)

and publication dried up except for a very rare book review in an undistinguished publication, and faculty members who serve on committees with Dr.
Jekyll report that the professor often doesn't show up for meetings or, when
present, contributes absolutely nothing of value.

Even more troubling, Dr. Jekyll has declined in collegiality, speaking dis-
dainfully to other faculty members, refusing to engage in common courtesies,
and often blocking departmental work by failing to show up at meetings or
completing assigned tasks. People have long been concerned and have put
Dr. Jekyll in touch with the institution's employee assistance program and
counseling center, but to no avail. Now the posttenure review committee has
to make a recommendation about Dr. Jekyll's future. Exactly half the members
have cast a negative vote. They argue that institutional policy requires the
committee to consider whether the faculty member has made sufficient progress since tenure, and that clearly hasn't been the case. Although the institution's policies state that a negative vote could allow the upper administration
to begin proceedings for the removal of tenure and subsequent dismissal,
these members believe that this type of shock treatment is precisely what Dr.
Jekyll needs.

The other half of the committee argues just as strongly that Dr. Jekyll
continues to add value to the university. The major international prize that Dr.
Jekyll won has become a major source of publicity for the university, and they
ask, "How will it look in the Chronicle of Higher Education if we fire the very
professor we always feature in our ads? Even if word gets out that we're
considering a negative vote, the result will be embarrassing." They argue that
the institutional focus of posttenure requires that they provide help to a faculty
member who needs it, and Dr. Jekyll clearly needs it. The deciding vote is
yours. What do you do?

1. Based simply on the information presented here, is your initial impulse to
   vote for a positive or a negative decision?
2. If the decision is ultimately positive, what recommendations would you
   make to Dr. Jekyll, and how would you present them?
3. If the decision is ultimately negative and you're appointed to present this
   result to Dr. Jekyll, how would you handle the meeting if he becomes
   angry and exhibits some of the uncollegial behavior described in the case
   study?

○ ○ ○

Another faculty member, Dr. Nobel, has placed you in a very different situation. By any measure, Dr. Nobel's performance has been phenomenal. Like Dr. Jekyll, Dr. Nobel won a prestigious international award shortly after becoming assistant professor. But unlike Dr. Jekyll, Dr. Nobel has amassed an almost unbelievable number of awards ever since. So it comes as a shock to you that the committee has presented you with a unanimously negative vote on Dr. Nobel's posttenure review. When you challenge the members of the committee, you discover that they are nitpicking about insignificant procedural mistakes that Dr. Nobel has made over the years, telling you nothing that seems to warrant a negative vote. You make a few discreet inquiries and discover that the rest of the faculty has long been jealous of Dr. Nobel and the professor's growing reputation. You suspect they may be using the posttenure review process to take him down a peg or two. You confront the committee with this hypothesis, and every member vehemently denies the accusation, restating the same minor problems they mentioned earlier. You go back to review the institution's policies for posttenure review and discover that as chair, you can't overturn their vote. The majority opinion becomes the recommendation of the committee as a whole. What do you do?

1. How do you attempt to redress what you regard as a blatant injustice?
2. What, if anything, do you tell Dr. Nobel since the policy states that discussions of the committee are to be kept confidential, with only the result and vote count conveyed to the faculty member?
3. How do you work to avoid a similar situation in the future?

o o o

You have just finished these difficult posttenure reviews when another faculty member, Dr. Darkside, shows up in your office and says, "Hi, you know that next year is my scheduled date for posttenure review, and I think I just don't want to go through all that. It could go pretty well, I suppose, but more likely I'll get a bunch of criticism about how I should've been doing this or should've been doing that. I don't see the point of that humiliation. So I thought I should tell you now that I'm going to go ahead and retire early so that I can save myself the trouble of gathering all those materials, having friends and colleagues scrutinize very personal things like student course evaluations, and then enduring their criticism." While you, of course, have not yet had an opportunity to examine Dr. Darkside's portfolio, you know that the general

(Continued)

consensus is that this professor is "pretty good but not great." What do you tell Dr. Darkside?

1. Would your response be any different if Dr. Darkside were in your own discipline, and you knew that since budget cuts are pending, you're likely to lose this line if Dr. Darkside retires?
2. If you could persuade Dr. Darkside to remain and go through the post-tenure review process, would you instruct the committee to do anything differently in light of this professor's sensitivity to criticism? Would it be fair to others to give the committee separate instructions in this case?
3. Would your response be any different if you were finishing your last year as chair of the posttenure review committee, and the chair-elect is a particularly blunt faculty member who is well known to "take no prisoners"?
4. How would you handle the situation if you persuaded Dr. Darkside to go through the process and it turned out to be as agonizing as the professor feared?

○ conclusion

Although the origins of posttenure review stemmed from an effort to eliminate deadwood from faculty ranks and increase productivity, a properly handled posttenure review can be a highly positive experience for both the faculty member and the reviewer. It provides an opportunity to celebrate past achievements and set new goals. It need not be excessively burdensome for the faculty member to prepare for. And it gives the institution an effective means of documenting that its tenure system works and that senior faculty members are contributing to the good of their students, school, and community.

References

American Association of University Professors. (1999). *Post-tenure review: An AAUP response*. Retrieved from http://www.aaup.org/AAUP/pubsres/policydocs/contents/PTR.htm.

Licata, C. M., & Morreale, J. C. (1999). Post-tenure review: National trends, questions and concerns. *Innovative Higher Education, 24*(1), 5–15.

O'Meara, K. A. (2004). Beliefs about post-tenure review: The influence of autonomy, collegiality, career stage, and institutional context. *Journal of Higher Education, 75*, 178–202.

Plater, W. M. (2001). A profession at risk: Using post-tenure review to save tenure and create an intentional future for academic community. *Change, 33*(4), 52–57.

Seldin, P. (1999). *Changing practices in evaluating teaching: A practical guide to improved faculty performance and promotion/tenure decisions.* San Francisco: Jossey-Bass/Anker.

Resources

Licata, C. M., & Morreale, J. C. (2005). *Post-tenure faculty review and renewal iii: Outcomes and impact.* Washington, DC: AAHE.

Licata, C. M., & Morreale, J. C. (2002). *Post-tenure faculty review and renewal: Experienced voices.* Washington, DC: AAHE.

Licata, C. M., & Morreale, J. C. (1997). *Post-tenure review: Policies, practices, precautions.* Washington, DC: AAHE.

Smith, D. N. (2011). Making the most of post-tenure review. *Academic Leadership.* http://www.academicleadership.org/423/making_the_most_of_post-tenure_review/.

part three

summative review and evaluation

7

merit evaluations

Merit evaluations, reviews conducted in order to determine the size of a faculty member's performance-based salary increase, are frequently included as part of the annual evaluations discussed in Chapter Four. Although these two processes often become fused in the minds of administrators, the focus of these reviews is quite different, so it's important to examine them separately.

As we've seen, an annual evaluation is largely a formative review that's integral to the institution's overall faculty development effort. It explores possible ways in which the person under review can build on what went well, address what didn't seem to be working, and develop meaningful goals for the future. A merit evaluation, however, has to be a summative review that's integral to the institution's overall faculty retention effort. It rewards the person under review for a high level of achievement and, like a raise that may come with a promotion, is intended to make salary reflect the faculty member's quality of performance. That is the theory, anyway, although like many well-intentioned administrative systems, merit increases have been fraught with challenges, inconsistencies, and unintended consequences (Manning, 1988). So before we can explore the best practices developed for this type of review, we first need to consider what some of these longstanding problems have been.

For one, most merit increase systems aren't funded in a manner that's either large enough or reliable enough to achieve the intended results. For instance, if supervisors had access to an annual pool of funding that was based on 10 to 15 percent of their personnel budgets, meaningful merit differentials could be made. Those whose teaching, research, and service had been extremely poor could receive no increase whatsoever. Star performers, the sort of faculty members who rise to national, even international, prominence, could receive increases of 20 percent or more. And the vast majority of faculty members could receive more modest increases that were still large enough to make a noticeable difference.

Such a system would mean that truly great faculty members would be less likely to seek employment elsewhere, while deadwood might be tempted to leave, and most of the faculty would earn a living wage. But most merit pools are very small—usually between 1 and 3 percent of the salary pool—and are inconsistent from year to year. During difficult economic times when no merit pool exists, administrators may have the best intentions of "making it up" to their best performers the next time raises become available, but it's extremely difficult to measure merit over the course of two, three, even four years. As a result, faculty members whose books happen to appear or grants happen to come in during a year when merit funding is available tend to win the salary lottery, while those whose work came to fruition a year or two earlier are frequently ignored. The result is an inconsistent application of merit increases and the unintended consequences of lowering morale among some of the very people the merit system was supposed to help.

Second, it becomes all but impossible to allocate meaningful merit increases from a pool of only about 1 to 3 percent of personnel costs. With small merit pools, well-intentioned efforts to reward good performance end up being disincentives for everyone. Those who do extremely well receive increases of only about 4 percent out of a 3 percent pool and think, "All that extra work and all I get is a lousy 1 percent extra? I'm not trying this hard again next year." Most faculty members receive a 3 percent increase and think, "All that work and all I get is the average increase? I'm *much* better than average, so I'm not trying this hard again next year." And those whose efforts were not very successful get 1 or 2 percent and think, "What's the point of trying in this system when I can't even get the average increase? I'm not trying this hard again next year." The result is that morale suffers across the board, and no one feels inspired to do better work. Once again, the merit pool ends up having an effect exactly opposite to what its designers had intended (Buller, 2009, 2011).

The third problem with merit-based salary systems is that defining merit and measuring it accurately are far more challenging than it initially appears. Faculty responsibilities vary widely from discipline to discipline. The number of student credit hours, refereed publications, and conference presentations that are reasonable to expect from a professor of history has no relevance at all to a professor of nursing, applied music, or exercise science, for example. Faculty members in traditional disciplines in the arts and sciences might be evaluated in part by the success of their undergraduate students when they enter graduate programs, but that metric is meaningless in more applied disciplines where baccalaureate students enter the workforce immediately after graduation. In other words, for every clear and objective metric one can develop for evaluating performance in certain disciplines, numerous examples can be found where the same approach won't work in other disciplines. As a result, it's difficult to compare apples to apples and eliminate much of the subjectivity that can result when making merit evaluations. The result often leads to appeals, grievances, and lawsuits even though the system was created in order to be fair and help the best faculty members.

Understanding that these problems exist provides a useful reminder to exert caution when working within a merit system, even though it may not be very useful if you're working at an institution where a certain approach to merit increases is required or if you're philosophically committed to the concept of pay for performance. As a result, how do you conduct merit evaluations, with all of their inherent problems, in the most equitable and efficient manner?

○ disentangling issues of merit from issues of equity

The first requirement in performing a fair and valid merit review is to disassociate questions of merit from those of inequity. Faculty members and even some administrators frequently confuse these two issues, but it's impossible to conduct an objective merit review without separating them. *Merit*, of course, is a judgment based on a person's performance. *Equity* is a judgment based on a person's just recompense.

In order to see the difference, consider a hypothetical situation that, while admittedly extreme, helps distinguish the two concepts. Faculty member A and faculty member B were both hired one year ago at the same institution in the same discipline with identical credentials and years of experience. Their letters of recommendation, interviews, and past performance all suggested that the two faculty members were equal in quality of work and achievement. Yet while faculty member A was hired at forty thousand dollars, faculty member B was given a salary of eighty thousand dollars. Now one year has gone by, and it's time to conduct merit evaluations that will be used for two purposes: to determine the amount of the faculty members' salary increase for the year and provide the first set of data for the promotion portfolios they'll be submitting in six years.

Faculty member A has had a good, strong year; in teaching, research, and service the minimum requirements of the discipline were all met, and you're not aware of any major problems or missteps associated with this faculty member. Faculty member B, however, has had an absolutely phenomenal year; the faculty member has quickly been recognized as a star teacher, submitted a successful grant application in record time, had several new contributions accepted for publication in the top-ranking journal of the discipline, and performed work on a committee that managed to bring a project that had long been stalled to a highly successful conclusion.

Equity considerations would suggest that you score faculty member A far ahead of faculty member B because, except for the past year, their records are far too comparable to justify such an extreme difference in salary. Merit considerations would suggest that you score faculty member B far ahead of faculty member A because no matter whether you consider only the past year or the entirety of their records, faculty member B has now performed at a much higher level than his or her colleague. In other words, if funds have been allocated to address salary inequity, it's clear that you'd use these to bring faculty member A up to an appropriate level. But if the goal of the evaluation is merit alone, then that salary differential must be set aside from your considerations, and matters of performance alone should drive your decision.

In actual situations, you're unlikely to encounter situations where salary inequity is so extreme or the level of prior performance so perfectly equal. But what this hypothetical situation does indicate is that no matter how much it may run counter to our deeply held notions of justice and overall fairness, merit evaluations can be conducted equitably only if the reviewer considers achievement alone and places no weight whatsoever on other factors.

If you approach the review by thinking, "What does this person deserve?" it becomes very easy to get merit and equity confused. A faculty member may deserve a highly positive review or a salary increase because he or she is underpaid relative to the amount of work that he or she does. Or another faculty member may deserve a highly positive review or a salary increase because of the truly outstanding performance that he or she gave during the period being evaluated. Those two considerations often lead to very different results, and if one department takes one approach and another department interprets merit differently, increased inequity will result. For this reason, unless the system in which you're operating specifically indicates that the same evaluation process is intended to address both merit and equity, it's very important to separate the two issues when making a summative judgment in a merit review. (For recommendations on how to proceed if you are addressing issues of inequity, see Buller, 2007, 2008.)

○ disentangling issues of merit from issues of worth

In a similar way to how merit decisions are often confused with equity decisions, the idea of merit often becomes blurred with the concept of worth. An activity may be meritorious—that is, it can be of extremely high quality—without reference to context or significance. *Worth* refers to how that activity adds value to the enterprise. So although the compensation systems of colleges and universities refer only to merit-based raises, evaluators can't help but consider both merit and worth in conjunction with each other.

What's an example of how a faculty member's work can be meritorious without also being worthwhile? The neuroscientist who publishes successful romance novels may be producing work of some merit (at least in terms of how many copies these books sell), but that activity is of peripheral interest to the discipline at best. Similarly, the academic who publishes reams of book reviews may have less of an impact on his or her field than the colleague whose single half-page research note revolutionizes the discipline. The difference bears some resemblance to the distinction between program assessment (which focuses on quality alone) and program review (which also addresses matters of sustainability and relevance to the institution's mission).

It may be too much to ask that the entire system of higher education revamp its approaches to merit pay in order to accommodate both merit and worth in their formulas but as an evaluator, you need to be aware of the distinction. Particularly when you're working with a review committee that becomes fixated on the quality of faculty activities alone, without any regard for their impact or significance, you can provide a useful corrective and direct the discussion toward how each individual adds worth to the unit and institution, albeit in different ways.

Determining Merit in a Complex Academic System

Even after issues of merit have been completely separated from issues of equity, it's often difficult for reviewers to evaluate the quality of one faculty member's performance relative to another because the roles and responsibilities of the faculty vary so widely in a complex academic system. In addition, many systems of merit evaluations are either overly prescriptive (counting publications, totaling the amount of grant support, relying on the scores of student course evaluations, and so on) or overly vague (stating that the reviewer should declare teaching, research, and service to be "unsatisfactory, adequate, superior, or exceptional," without providing clear guidance about how those terms are to be used). It can be sufficiently challenging to determine what constitutes exceptional research in a single department, since the types of scholarship that various faculty members pursue are likely to assume many different forms, but this difficulty is compounded immeasurably if you serve as a member of a review committee at the college or institutional level. What, for instance, is there in common among a multimillion-dollar grant from the National Institutes of Health, a solo art exhibit, a textbook, a series of publications in *Science* and *Nature*, a performance as part of a piano duo, a successful business plan, and a monograph of historical research published by a prestigious university press? How could you explain to someone the similarity in superb teaching by a lecturer, a seminar leader, a lab supervisor, an athletic coach, a studio musician, and an internship mentor?

Since your procedures themselves may not tell you everything you want to know about how to evaluate faculty members fairly when they have very different assignments, the following suggestions may make the process both easier for you and more equitable for those who are being reviewed.

Establish the evaluation rubric before you begin to examine applications

Just as in teaching we can end up grading students unfairly if we establish standards only as we are reading their papers, so can merit determinations end up being inconsistent unless you understand in advance what you're looking for. If you alone are conducting the merit evaluation, as department chairs often do, decide in advance what level of achievement you'll be looking for in order to justify each level of rating. (And when the process is over, start working with your department to establish uniform standards that can provide a basis for these evaluations in the future.) If you're part of a review committee, try to develop consensus about the criteria you'll be using before you consider the first portfolio. This conversation will remind committee members of the importance of applying standards consistently in different disciplines. You'll also produce results that can be defended more easily in the case of challenges and appeals.

Consult commonly accepted sources about appropriate forms of research in different disciplines

You don't have to reinvent the wheel when deciding which forms of research are regarded as most appropriate in different disciplines, which journals are considered most prestigious, and which alternative forms of scholarship are accepted as most suitable for disseminating scholarship in specific fields. Diamond and Adam (1995, 2000) provide valuable insight into the most relevant sources and criteria to use when measuring the effectiveness of a faculty member's teaching, research, and service in a wide variety of academic areas. The Eigenfactor, the ISI's Impact Factor, and Scopus's Source Normalized Impact per Paper, which were mentioned in the last chapter, can be used in scientific disciplines to measure the effect of a faculty member's research on his or her peers. Frameworks for evaluating alternative forms of scholarship have been proposed or critiqued by Fiddler, McGury, Marienau, Rogers, and Scheideman (1996), O'Meara (2006), Adams, Rust, and Brinthaupt (2011), Peek and Pomerantz (1998), and Albers (2006, 2007).

Without examining objective discussions about what constitutes valid scholarship and standards of excellence in disciplines different from ours, we too readily evaluate a faculty member's work in terms of how we do our own research, a practice that can lead us to draw false or incomplete conclusions. A historian may ask, "Why don't these artists ever publish anything?" while a scientist may ask, "Why don't these historians ever bring in grant support?"

Evaluate teaching based on impact and progress, not on the professor's popularity or the students' level of ability

Ever since Robert Barr and John Tagg published their landmark article about university education in *Change* magazine in 1995, the emphasis throughout American higher education has shifted from how well professors teach to how well students learn. That shift in focus has produced a commendable improvement in the way that colleges and universities assess the effectiveness of their programs. It does, however, create certain challenges when evaluating the merit of individual instructors. For example, if a discipline or an entire institution decides that meritorious professors will be those who bring about the greatest progress in their students' performance, what do you do in the case of the teacher whose upper-level course consists solely of students who reach the course when they're already well trained, highly motivated, and without very much additional progress to make? What do you do about the professor who, try as hard as he or she might, ultimately can't motivate a class to learn because the students who happen to be in that course are completely disengaged with the material? In addition, if teaching effectiveness is based largely or solely on student evaluations, how do you compensate for the halo effect—the phenomenon that causes popular professors (or professors who teach popular subjects) to receive higher scores in all areas than those who teach widely disliked material in courses that students have to take? (See Clayson and Haley, 2011.)

For all of these reasons, the most important question a reviewer can ask when trying to evaluate the effectiveness of teaching is, "Since neither student course evaluations nor value-added learning assessments are likely to give me the information I need, what will?" The answer to this question will vary somewhat by discipline and institution, but is likely to include peer evaluation, 360-degree reviews, comparison of student performance and evaluation scores to those of colleagues teaching similar courses under similar conditions, and direct observation by the reviewer himself or herself.

The Lake Wobegon Effect

On the radio program *Prairie Home Companion*, Garrison Keillor ends his stories about the fictional town of Lake Wobegon, Minnesota, by calling the community a place where "all the women are strong, all the men are good looking, and all the children are above average." In evaluations where, due to grade inflation or other factors that skew the score, more than half the people under review are rated as above average, this shift of results toward the high end of the scale is known as "the Lake Wobegon effect." (See, for example, Haley, Johnson, and McGee, 2010; Kruger, 1999; Cannell, 1989; and Carney, 1991.)

Many administrators, trustees, legislators, and community citizens believe they're witnessing this effect in faculty merit evaluations. "How can so many of them be rated as 'excellent'?" they ask. "The terms *superior* and *excellent* are used so loosely in matters of faculty merit that they really don't mean anything." As a result, institutions are frequently encouraged and occasionally compelled to recalibrate their faculty evaluation scales in order to make the results adhere to the standard bell-shaped curve. But that type of distribution simply doesn't work for faculty merit evaluations, and reviewers need to be aware of those reasons in order to conduct fair reviews.

A bell-shaped distribution makes perfect sense when you are evaluating a random assortment of individuals. Throw the names of everyone from a particular state or region into a hat, draw five hundred of those names, teach them some new concept or skill that none of them already knows, grade them on their performance, and the result is likely to fall into a bell-shaped pattern. But the faculty of a college or university is not a random selection of individuals. To begin with, all faculty members have to undergo a rigorous period of training and evaluation before they're even offered a position. Then they're reviewed annually and undergo particularly thorough evaluations when being considered for tenure or promotion. Even afterward, with the spread of posttenure review throughout much of higher education, their performance is likely to be placed under strict scrutiny on a regular basis thereafter. Because of these multiple evaluation processes, those who are below average—and, at many colleges and universities, even those who are merely average—aren't retained; they're eliminated from the system at the earliest opportunity. So although it may be possible to talk about an institutional average for performance, that average shouldn't be misconstrued as performing only at a middling level of quality.

What this lopsided variation in distribution means for a person performing a merit review in higher education is that unless the rating scale is specifically adjusted for use in an academic setting, the results are likely to skew toward the higher end. That's not a flaw in the system; it's a reflection of how faculty members are trained, selected, retained, and rewarded. For this reason, it's usually not helpful to begin a round of merit evaluations by thinking that you need to confine your ratings of faculty members to balance at the middle of the scale. For example, if your rating system is the type of A to F grading scale that we discussed in Chapter Two, and you try to make those grades average out to be a C, you'll probably be rating people too low. If the hiring and evaluation processes are functioning properly at your institution, you may well not have anyone who is performing at the level of a D or F. You may not even have anyone who's performing only at the level of a C. Like the children of Lake Wobegon, everyone is likely to be above average. What this skewing means is that for merit evaluations, you're more likely to be considering gradations of good performance rather that a range that spans every category from Excellent to Completely Unsatisfactory.

Consider the following differences. Think of the faculty members in your program and, without even looking at their résumés or annual reports, try to classify all of them by placing each person in one of these five categories:

1. Very good
2. Good
3. Satisfactory
4. Less than satisfactory
5. Completely unacceptable

In most cases, you'll end up with one of two results: either everyone will collect at the top of the scale, with very few people in the bottom two categories, or you'll find yourself ranking people as "less than satisfactory" and "completely unacceptable" even though their performance really has not been that poor.

Next, try this experiment again, but this time use the following five categories:

1. Stellar
2. Very good
3. Good
4. Meets expectations
5. Below expectations

Think of the term *stellar* as referring to the faculty member who has had a truly phenomenal year: a major new book of research has come out, a large grant proposal was funded, a major national or international award was received, or something similar occurred. Think of the rating *very good* as referring to the faculty member whose year doesn't fall into the category of being stellar but who has surpassed the normally high standards that he or she typically meets. Think of the term *good* as referring to a person who is likely to have received strong course evaluations from students and peers, performed significant research, and gone above and beyond the expected level of service on committees, to the discipline, and in professional associations. Think of the ranking *meets expectations* as referring to someone who probably has fulfilled all the basic requirements of the institution and discipline (and those requirements are already quite demanding) but who is likely not to have done much than go beyond his or her customarily solid performance. Think of the rating *below expectations* as referring to the faculty member who truly has failed to work at the level that the discipline requires, is likely to have relatively low scores in student and peer evaluations of teaching, or whose research does not seem to have been very productive.

When most people approach merit reviews in this way, they find that their evaluations become far more nuanced and objective. They're rating people's work by distinguishing various levels of effective performance rather than trying to force people into categories like Average, Below Average, and Failing.

Tying Merit to Institutional Priorities

While the merit system in use at your institution may be so prescriptive that no flexibility is possible, in other cases it can be beneficial to link these degrees of distinction to the school's goals, mission or vision statement, strategic plan, or community code. For example, the mission statement of Armstrong Atlantic State University reads, "Armstrong is teaching-centered and student-focused, providing diverse learning experiences and professional programs grounded in the liberal arts." Key principles outlined in this university's statements of vision and values include a commitment to "education that is student-focused, . . . balance among teaching, mentoring, and scholarship, . . . [and] civic engagement through outreach and service." What's distinctive about these statements is that the word *research* doesn't appear in any of them. (See http://www.armstrong.edu/About/armstrong_facts/mission _statement.) Among Armstrong's five strategic goals, two have to do with teaching, and one each involves technology, financial sustainability, and visibility. In none of these goals is there a focus on research or scholarship. (See http://www.armstrong.edu/About/armstrong_facts/ about_strategic_plan.) That type of institutional identity sends a clear signal about how merit should be evaluated. At a teaching-first university, the quality of teaching and the success of student learning should be paramount, with service to the community a secondary but still important goal. If you were a reviewer at this university attempting to distinguish gradations of merit between two extremely accomplished professors, the superlative teacher who happens to be a good researcher will thus be given priority to the superlative researcher who happens to be a good teacher.

Quite a different conclusion might be drawn at Tohoku University in Japan, where the mission statement proclaims the school to be a "research-first" institution and every reference to teaching in the school's mission statement and historical summary also discusses research: "The faculty's cutting edge research will be reflected in their teaching" and "scholars . . . [will] not only pursue highly productive research but . . . also put their findings to work in the teaching of their students" (http://www.tohoku.ac.jp/english/profile/about/02/about0201/).

In most cases, an institution's mission will not be delineated in such black-and-white terms. But the emphasis that's outlined in its mission or vision statement does provide guidance into which achievements are regarded as most significant. For this reason, as you plan your review, you might consider questions like the following:

1. To what extent did this faculty member's accomplishments reflect the *mission* of the institution and of his or her discipline?
2. To what extent did this faculty member's accomplishments move the institution and his or her discipline forward in fulfilling the goals of the *strategic plan*?
3. To what extent did this faculty member's accomplishments advance the institution and his or her discipline toward attaining their stated *visions*?
4. To what extent did this faculty member's accomplishments fall into those areas deemed most significant by the institution's fundamental *principles or values*?
5. To what extent did this faculty member's accomplishments serve the *stakeholders* regarded by this institution as most significant?

Notice that these questions don't help you determine whether a given faculty member's performance was excellent, but they do direct you toward the factors to consider when making that determination. You'll need to make sure that your school's policies permit these criteria to be used in merit evaluations, as well as your supervisor's level of support for conducting merit evaluations in this way. At most schools, this approach won't be a problem and may well be strongly encouraged. As Larry Braskamp and John Ory have said (1994), "A faculty member's value is context-dependent, taking into account institutional expectations and his or her career stage" (p. 64). In other words, an institution's focus and future direction play a legitimate role in evaluating a faculty member's merit. Nevertheless, as in any other type of evaluation, don't base your review on any factor that can't be defended if a challenge or appeal is filed.

---

mini-case studies: merit evaluations

You work at an institution where the policies require you to assign each faculty member to one of the following five categories: Exemplary, Good, Satisfactory, Needs Improvement, and Unsatisfactory. These policies also state that the Exemplary category is to be used only rarely, denoting individuals who have truly excelled on a world-class level. The Good category is reserved for faculty members whose performance in the past year exceeded their typically high level of quality, Satisfactory indicates those who have fully satisfied the expectations of the institution and discipline, Needs Improvement for those whose performance didn't meet standards but could be enhanced through mentoring and faculty development, and Unsatisfactory for those whose work has continuously or egregiously failed to meet expected standards and thus should be considered for termination.

You find these categories far too narrow for most purposes and have repeatedly voiced your opposition to them, but you're required to use them. As you review the performance of one of your faculty members, Professor Marginal, you note that this year his performance has slipped a bit and thus has not "fully satisfied the expectations of the institution and discipline." But you can't honestly say that Professor Marginal's performance "could be enhanced through mentoring and faculty development." You've tried these measures before, and Marginal just keeps plodding along, doing the bare minimum to get by and not a bit more.

In which category does Marginal's merit fall this year? You can safely assume that he's neither Exemplary nor Good, but which of the remaining three rankings seems most appropriate?

(Continued)

- If you select Satisfactory, how do you respond to your supervisor when asked to justify this decision since this year Professor Marginal did not fully satisfy the expectations of the institution and discipline?
- If you select Needs Improvement, how do you respond to the faculty delegation who shows up in your office protesting that history has shown Professor Marginal's performance to be impervious to mentoring and faculty development?
- If you select Unsatisfactory, how do you respond when Professor Marginal angrily informs you that he has neither continuously nor egregiously failed to meet expected standards and is outraged that he'll now need to defend himself in termination proceedings?

○ ○ ○

You work in a very strange environment in which all three professors whom you have to evaluate for merit increases this year earn precisely eighty thousand dollars. The institution has allocated you a 1 percent salary pool (eight hundred dollars) that you are required to distribute according to the faculty member's "meritorious performance." What complicates this situation is that due to dismal budgets, this merit pool is the first salary increase funding that the faculty has seen in six years. Using your institution's standards for evaluating merit, you find Dr. A's work to have been exceptional, Dr. B's work to have met but not exceeded expectations, and Dr. C's work to have been slightly below the expectations of the institution and discipline. How do you allocate your merit pool?

- If you give it all to Dr. A, what do you say to Dr. B and Dr. C who have not had a raise in six years and whose performance, while not as strong as Dr. A's, was not poor or seriously deficient by any reasonable standard?
- If you give any increase at all to Dr. C, how do you reply to Dr. A and Dr. B when they protest that the funding was specifically allocated for merit, but Dr. C's performance failed to meet the expectations of the institutions?
- If you give a portion of the money (either equal or unequal shares) to Dr. A and Dr. B, how do you answer Dr. A, who claims that a single increase

in six years was hard enough to bear without having to share a "measly eight hundred dollars" with a faculty member whose performance never rose above the level of "meeting expectations"?

○ ○ ○

You are serving as a member of a committee charged with apportioning merit increases to the faculty. The first committee member says that because all faculty members under review are meritorious, the funding should be allocated in such a way that each faculty member receives the same percentage. The second committee member agrees with the first but insists that the funding be distributed in equal dollar amounts. The third committee member says that because the institution defines itself as a teaching-first university, larger increases should be given to those who demonstrated superior teaching through student and peer reviews, the success of their students in subsequent courses, and the completion of an exemplary teaching portfolio. The fourth committee member argues that the designation "teaching first" means something quite different from "teaching only," and that the money should be apportioned in such a way that excellent teachers who also have solid achievements in research and service should receive a larger increase. The fifth committee member suggests that since the institution's mission statement follows its commitment to teaching first with a secondary commitment to civic engagement, priority should go to faculty members who were able to use community service learning and civic engagement projects to improve their teaching. The sixth committee member is adamant that the determination of excellence in teaching is a purely subjective matter and that more objective criteria should be used to allocate the money.

You're the seventh committee member. If you side with any of the other six, that procedure will be used, and you'll need to have strong arguments to counter those in favor of the other five approaches. If you propose a seventh approach, the whole committee will be at an impasse. What do you do? Do you see any way to achieve a compromise by combining two or more of the other approaches?

○ conclusion

Since merit evaluations are typically conflated with annual reviews, the advice in this chapter should be considered alongside that in Chapter Four. In addition, reviewers should try whenever possible to adopt evaluation standards that would yield the same result regardless of who the reviewer is. Although the concept of merit is equated in most academic settings with the person's professional performance during the review period just completed, it's impossible for most people to separate the idea of merit with that of their "worth" or "value" as a person. For this reason, clear definition of terms and a certain degree of understanding or sensitivity are highly desirable when reporting the results of a merit review to a faculty member.

References

Adams, C. L., Rust, D. Z., & Brinthaupt, T. M. (2011). Evolution of a peer review and evaluation program for online course development. In J. E. Miller & J. E. Groccia (Eds.), *To improve the academy*. San Francisco: Jossey-Bass.

Albers, C. (2006). Revising policy to recognize diverse forms of scholarship. In J. Fanghanel & D. Warren (Eds.), *Proceedings of the International Conference on the Scholarship of Teaching and Learning: 2005–2006*. London: Centre for Education and Alternative Practices.

Albers, C. (2007). Developing a shared meaning of scholarship to enable the revision of promotion policy. *International Journal for the Scholarship of Teaching and Learning, 1*(1). Retrieved from http://academics.georgiasouthern.edu/ijsotl/2007_v1n1.htm.

Barr, R. B., & Tagg, J. (1995). From teaching to learning: A new paradigm for undergraduate education. *Change, 27*(6), 12–25.

Braskamp, L. A., & Ory, J. C. (1994). *Assessing faculty work: Enhancing individual and institutional performance*. San Francisco: Jossey-Bass.

Buller, J. L. (2007). Addressing issues of faculty salary inequity. *Department Chair, 18*(2), 17–20.

Buller, J. L. (2008). Dealing with market inequity in faculty salaries. *Academic Leader, 24*(5), 3,7.

Buller, J. L. (2009). The pros and cons of merit pay. *Academic Leader, 25*(6), 7–8.

Buller, J. L. (2011). Promoting research while advancing instruction, part 1. *Academic Leader, 27*(1), 3, 7.

Cannell, J. J. (1989). The Lake Wobegon effect revisited. *Educational Measurement: Issues and Practice, 7*(4), 12–15.

Carney, R. (1991). The "Lake Wobegon effect": Implications for the assessment of exceptional children. *Journal of School Psychology, 29*, 183–186.

Clayson, D., & Haley, D. A. (2011). Are students telling the truth? A critical look at the student evaluation of teaching. *Marketing Education Review, 21*, 101–112.

Diamond, R. M., & Adam, B. E. (Eds.). (1995). *The disciplines speak: Rewarding the scholarly, professional, and creative work of faculty.* Washington, DC: American Association for Higher Education.

Diamond, R. M., & Adam, B. E. (Eds.). (2000). *The disciplines speak II: More statements on rewarding the scholarly, professional, and creative work of faculty.* Washington, DC: American Association for Higher Education.

Fiddler, M., McGury, S., Marienau, C., Rogers, R., & Scheideman, W. (1996). Broadening the scope of scholarship: A suggested framework. *Innovative Higher Education, 21*, 127–139.

Haley, M. R., Johnson, M., & McGee, M. K. (2010). A framework for reconsidering the Lake Wobegon effect. *Journal of Economic Education, 41*, 95–109.

Kruger, J. (1999). Lake Wobegon be gone! The "below-average effect" and the egocentric nature of comparative ability judgments. *Journal of Personality and Social Psychology, 77*, 221–223.

Manning, R. C. (1988). *The teacher evaluation handbook: Step-by-step techniques and forms for improving instruction.* Upper Saddle River, NJ: Prentice Hall.

O'Meara, K. A. (2006). Encouraging multiple forms of scholarship in faculty reward systems: Have academic cultures really changed? *New Directions for Institutional Research, 129*, 77–95.

Peek, R. P., & Pomerantz, J. P. (1998). Electronic scholarly journal publishing. *Annual Review of Information Science and Technology, 33*, 321–356.

Resources

Berber, M. A. (1974). Professors, performance, and rewards. *Industrial Relations, 13*(1), 69–77.

8

tenure evaluations

Tenure is sometimes described as the academic equivalent of marriage. While it's certainly possible that the union will be dissolved by "divorce," everyone starts off with the assumption that the relationship is "for keeps." The metaphor isn't perfect, of course. Far more marriages end in divorce than tenured faculty members are dismissed from colleges and universities. And while matrimony is intended to last all the way "until death do you part," tenure lasts only until the faculty member chooses to retire. Yet despite differences, there's one aphorism that works just as well if you substitute the word *tenure* for *marry*: tenure in haste; repent at leisure.

When faculty members receive tenure at an institution, they are likely to remain there for a very long time. Not only does tenure represent a significant investment of resources, but it also shapes the personality of the institution. If you tenure the right people, your program will have a solid core of talent that can survive all the vicissitudes that may occur. But if you tenure the wrong people, your institution will suffer, and you'll have made a decision that you'll regret for many years to come.

○ a brief history of tenure

Although based on ideas as old as universities themselves, the concept of tenure, as we currently understand it, has identifiable American origins. As James Shannahan (1973) notes,

> Possibly the first tenure legislation in America was an act passed by Massachusetts in 1886. This act allowed districts to employ teachers for periods longer than one year. Tenure had its origin in the United States in the informal practices and local regulations which established it in cities and school districts. The District of Columbia in 1906 provided district-wide tenure. The first state with a law of general application was New Jersey in 1909 [p. 276].

As the twentieth century continued and other aspects of university life—such as semester length, the development of the academic major, and standardized units such as the student credit hour—became more universal, professors and administrators saw the need to regularize policies on tenure and academic freedom as well:

> In the wake of Vanderbilts, Rockefellers, and Stanfords who forged new universities with their amassed wealth, an empowered faculty, who were themselves now making important contributions to the industrialization of western society, needed a shield to ensure the integrity of their teaching and research [Loope, 1995, p. 3].

Such thoughts led to the founding of the American Association of University Professors (AAUP) in 1915 and to the creation of that group's first Declaration of Principles. This original declaration established a fairly long probationary period for faculty members:

> In every institution there should be an unequivocal understanding as to the term of each appointment; and the tenure of professorships and associate professorships, and of all positions above the grade of instructor after ten years of service, should be permanent (subject to the provisions hereinafter given for removal upon charges) [American Association of University Professors, 1915].

That period was reduced to seven years when the 1915 declaration was amended as the Statement of Principles on Academic Freedom and Tenure in 1940 (http://www.aaup.org/AAUP/pubsres/policydocs/contents/1940statement.htm). A seven-year limit on tenure-track positions has become the de facto standard at most American colleges and universities ever since. Nevertheless, until the 1960s, most tenure decisions were purely administrative matters. "In 1959, however, only 26 of 80 institutions surveyed involved faculty in tenure recommendations" (American Council on Education, American Association of University Professors, and United Educators Insurance Risk Retention Group, 2000, p. 27). As the professoriate took a more activist position in asserting its rights of protecting academic freedom through tenure, administrative tenure procedures at most American institutions ultimately came to be replaced almost universally by shared governance in tenure procedures.

The value of tenure in protecting academic freedom is frequently cited when threats to the positions of specific faculty members—such as occurred during the McCarthy era, the Vietnam War, and the period immediately after 9/11—were taking place. Yet others have argued that tenure has additional benefits as well. Both John Silber (1989), a former president of Boston University, and Henry Rosovsky (1991), a former dean of the faculty of arts and sciences at Harvard, defend tenure on the basis of its being a highly desirable employment benefit and part of a university's "social contract" with professors. Just as institutions use salaries, start-up funds, and attractive schedules to lure the best professors into affiliating with them, so is the security and "family relationship" that results from tenure a factor in making a professor want to work at one institution rather than another.

Yet despite the ardent defenders of tenure, attacks on it have been numerous in recent years, frequently led by governing boards or state legislators who see tenure as a policy that protects poorly performing faculty members, limits the ability of institutions to adjust their staffing to meet unanticipated needs, "and discriminates against new and innovative faculty" (Snyder, 2000, p. 103). The result, exacerbated by a host of financial concerns, has led to a greater reliance on adjunct faculty, instructors under annual contracts, and other substitutes for the type of academic tenure promoted by the AAUP. For example, Lindenwood University in Missouri abolished tenure in 1994. "In 1995, the South Carolina legislature examined, but did not pass, a bill to abolish tenure at public institutions" (Trower, 2000, p. 24). When Florida Gulf Coast University began offering classes in 1997, it was designed and created as an institution that would hire faculty members on multiyear contracts rather than tenure. (One group of faculty members, who transferred to the university from the University of South Florida, Fort Myers, was allowed to retain its tenure status.) In a survey of U.S. university presidents in 2011, more them half of them favored systems that did not include traditional tenure. (See Stripling, 2011.) Hence, since tenure as a concept is increasingly under attack, it's all the more important that tenure review committees perform their task professionally, equitably, and with full accountability.

○ what tenure is and is not

The definition of *tenure* varies somewhat by institution. For example, at the University of Illinois, the Office of Human Resources states that "tenure refers to the indefinite length of some appointments." This definition is slightly expanded at the University of Texas Southwest Medical Center, where tenure is defined as "a status of continuing appointment as a member of the faculty" (http://www.utsouthwestern.edu/utsw/cda/dept237881/files/250817.html#what%20is%20tenure?) and much more fully at the University of Colorado Boulder where tenure is equated with "a contract for continuous employment with the university until resignation or retirement, subject to certain conditions" (http://www.colorado.edu/aar/tenure/Definitions.htm).

Based on these and other common definitions, we might summarize the definition of tenure as a faculty member's privilege of anticipating continued employment at an institution until the time of resignation or retirement unless terminated for financial exigency, program closure, or cause (see, for example, Amacher and Meiners, 2004). If we approach tenure in this way, there are two key factors in this definition.

First, whereas tenure is commonly referred to as a faculty member's right, it is more technically termed a privilege. Rights are given to everyone and cannot be lost except under highly severe or unusual circumstances; privileges must be earned and can be forfeited under a much broader range of circumstances. In this way, we refer to the *right* of life, liberty, and the pursuit of happiness, but the *privilege* of holding a driver's license, passport, or public office. Since tenure must be earned and can be revoked, it falls into the category of being a privilege.

Second, there are three common grounds for revoking tenure. *Financial exigency* occurs when a budgetary crisis is severe enough to make it impossible for the institution to meet its contractual obligations. *Program closure* exists when, because of enrollment demand or the change in institutional focus, the discipline in which the faculty member works is no longer needed at the institution, and reasonable assignment of the faculty member is impossible. *Cause* exists when the institution concludes that individuals have broken the terms of their contracts by engaging in inappropriate actions "related, directly and substantially, to the fitness of faculty members in their professional capacities as teachers or researchers" (http://www.aaup.org/AAUP/pubsres/policydocs/contents/RIR.htm).

Two U.S. Court of Appeals cases upheld institutional authority to terminate tenured faculty members even in the absence of any express contractual provision granting such authority. The first case, *Krotkoff v. Goucher College* (1978), concerned a termination due to a bona-fide financial exigency; the second case, *Jimenez v. Almodovar* (1981), dealt with a termination due to discontinuance of an academic program. Both cases resort to academic custom and usage to imply terms that are not specifically stated in the faculty contract. Both cases also identify implicit rights of tenured faculty members that limit the institution's termination authority (Kaplin and Lee, 2006).

For each ground (or "cause") included in its dismissal policy, the institution should also include a definition of that ground, along with the criteria or standards for applying the definition to particular cases. (The AAUP statement may serve this purpose for the "unethical conduct" ground.) Since such definitions and criteria may become part of the institution's contract with faculty members, they should be drafted clearly and specifically enough, and applied sensitively enough, to avoid contract interpretation problems (Kaplin and Lee, 2006).

The implications of these factors are that tenured faculty members are entitled to two privileges that are not available for temporary, untenured, short-term contract, or non-tenure-track faculty members. First, they are entitled to be told the reason why their services are no longer required, with the expectation that those reasons will be related to financial exigency, program closure, or cause. Faculty members without tenure are considered to be working on term contracts, and term contract employees don't have any legitimate expectation of continued employment when that contract ends. The comparison that's often made is that a term contract faculty member is employed under conditions similar to those of a worker you hire to paint your house. Once the house is painted, the contract is at an end, and the worker has no reason to expect continued employment. The next time you hire a painter, you're free to hire the same worker or someone else without any obligation to provide a reason for that decision.

Second, tenured faculty members are entitled to be given due process to challenge that decision. The type of due process the person is given depends on the nature, size, and tradition of the institution. It need not be a "trial"; it need not even be a formal hearing. But the faculty member must be allowed to appeal the revocation of tenure by providing evidence that the reason given is untrue or inadequate. That appeal may be reviewed by a board, panel, or single administrator, but the faculty member does have some right of appeal.

Therefore, despite perceptions to the contrary, tenure does not make it impossible for an institution to terminate faculty members who are incompetent, fail to meet contract obligations, or commit inappropriate actions that make their continuance at the institution untenable. They can also be dismissed if their entire program is eliminated, and there is nowhere else at the institution where their services are needed, or if the college or university is in danger of closing or otherwise not meeting its primary obligations to students and other stakeholders should the faculty members remain on the payroll. Nevertheless, all three of these scenarios involve extreme actions taken under the most calamitous of situations. So while it's not proper to think, "Once we tenure these faculty members, it's absolutely impossible to terminate them," it's also not proper to think, "Let's go ahead and tenure these faculty members because we can always give a reason and dismiss them if that proves to be a poor decision." Tenuring someone, like marrying someone, is a serious matter "not to be entered into unadvisedly or lightly, but reverently, deliberately, and in accordance with the purposes for which [the practice] was instituted (Church of England, 2004, p. 423).

○ why the difference between tenure and promotion decisions matters

As we'll see in Chapter Nine, promotion evaluations are based almost exclusively on what a person has accomplished. They're necessarily backward looking because their goal is to determine whether an individual has achieved enough to merit inclusion among the next higher rank of the professoriate. Tenure evaluations, however, are based largely on a person's potential. The guide *Making Tenure Decisions: Philosophy, Criteria, and Expectations* (n.d.), developed at the University of Wyoming, describes the decision:

> *A decision about tenure is a decision about the future, not about the past.* The essential question to be answered is this: Does the candidate's record reflect both the commitment and the promise to sustain a career-long record of effective teaching and advising, scholarship at the forefronts of knowledge, and effective service? . . . [A] tenure decision is a forecast. We ought to ask whether the candidate has

established the momentum needed for two or three more decades' worth of strong contributions to the university's mission [pp. 2–3].

Another way of phrasing that key question is, "Will this person probably continue to excel at a level that makes him or her a desirable member of our faculty for the long term?" Posing the question in this way may make it sound as though you're trying to predict the future, and in many ways you are. You're trying to figure out whether this faculty member will be a good fit for the institution for a number of years to come. Of course, the only basis you have to make that judgment is the faculty member's past performance, and as they say in investment commercials, past performance is not a reliable indicator of future results. In other words, you may be left asking two questions: "If I can't really trust past performance in a tenure decision, then am I just making a guess?" and, "If I do base tenure decisions on past performance, then isn't this review really identical to a promotion evaluation?" The answer to both of these questions is no, and to illustrate why that's the case, consider a hypothetical situation.

We'll start with the second question and rephrase it as, "How is a tenure decision different from a promotion decision?" Let's imagine that you are reviewing a faculty member who has published three well-received works of research, brought the institution more than $8 million in successful grant proposals, and published a dozen peer-reviewed articles in highly regarded journals. On the basis of this level of scholarly production, does this faculty member deserve promotion to the rank of associate professor? At most institutions, the answer would be yes. That level of scholarly achievement clearly meets or exceeds the expectations most schools have for someone to enter the rank of associate professor.

But then let's ask, "On the basis of this level of scholarly production, does this faculty member deserve tenure?" Here the honest answer is, "It depends." For example, if this assistant professor came to the institution with a Ph.D. newly in hand and accomplished everything described earlier during his or her six-year probationary period, then almost certainly even a very prestigious institution would say that the faculty member has passed the bar in research for being granted tenure. But if all of these achievements were accomplished twenty years ago with almost no scholarly activity in the interim, then very few institutions are likely to be willing to risk a positive tenure vote. The faculty member may still deserve to receive the rank of associate professor, since the achievements for promotion tend to be cumulative, but tenure decisions are more often based on patterns of achievement than collective achievements alone.

The situations you actually encounter are unlikely to be as extreme as that described in this hypothetical example. More commonly, you'll be dealing with faculty members who accomplish relatively little for several years and then have a burst of activity as the tenure review nears. The key question in that case will be, "How likely is this faculty member to continue this high rate of activity after tenure is granted?" If you don't have good reasons for supposing that the faculty member's recent productivity will persist—such as might occur if the faculty member works in a field where research projects take several years to come to fruition, has had access to a suitable research environment for only a short time, or faced significant obstacles, now overcome, that legitimately prevented this scholarship from being completed earlier—then this candidate may be someone whose work intensifies only in the face of an immediate deadline. Tenuring faculty members like that can be problematic. Institutions can find themselves with an abundance of "career associate professors" (or even "career assistant professors" in systems where tenure and promotion decisions are not linked) who will never reach a higher rank.

There's a second reason that tenure and promotion decisions are different: faculty members who leave one institution for another almost always take their rank with them; it is far rarer for faculty members to be allowed to transfer their tenure status. For this reason, promotion decisions have to be made in the context of academic standards across institutions: Will an associate professor here, for instance, have reasonably similar credentials to an associate professor at a peer institution? But tenure can be a more localized matter for the specific institution. At a school where the mission gives priority to the quality of instruction, it may make perfect sense to tenure a faculty member who's a spectacular teacher but doesn't have the scholarly credentials to receive tenure at another institution with a strong research mission. Similarly, universities that place emphasis on research may tenure a faculty member who is completely ineffective in the classroom because teaching will not be a significant part of that person's responsibilities. What all this means is that tenure review committees must give serious consideration to the school's individual mission and focus in order to determine whether applicants are a good fit for that environment. As we've seen, superb teaching skills may easily outweigh mediocre research at a university that gives primacy to the success and intellectual growth of undergraduate students. That same case is unlikely to be successful at an institution that is either in or soon aspires to be in the Carnegie Institution's highest classification for doctorate-granting institutions with very high research activity.

Finally, the third difference between tenure and promotion decisions arises from their impact on faculty members. Negative promotion decisions usually mean "not now." Negative tenure decisions usually mean "not at all." For example, most academic systems allow a faculty member who goes up for promotion to the rank of professor but is unsuccessful to apply again in future years. Yet in tenure cases, negative decisions lead to terminal contracts. A study performed by Michael Dooris (2002) found that "those who did not achieve tenure generally had ended their university employment, although a very few continued employment in nontenured positions such as staff jobs"(p. 90). Tenure decisions are therefore a bit like capital punishment cases: if you decide against someone unjustly, you may well not have an opportunity to remedy that mistake. As a result, it's not only important for tenure decisions to be based on scrupulous attention to high academic standards; they must also be based on the most equitable practices we can devise.

○ incorporating both rigor and fairness into tenure evaluations

The AAUP recommends four major strategies to make tenure decisions both meaningful and fair:

1. *All standards and procedures should be clear to each applicant.* As we saw in Chapter Six, it's a poor pedagogical procedure to grade students according to a rubric of which they're unaware. In a similar manner, it's inappropriate to evaluate faculty members according to standards and procedures that haven't been fully explained to them. Throughout a faculty member's probationary period, it's important for someone, such as the department chair or the head of the promotion and tenure committee, to describe in detail how the faculty member will be evaluated for tenure and the criteria that will be used in making that decision. The faculty member should also be given a written copy of these standards and procedures, with a signed memorandum retained, verifying that the person has received and read them.

2. *Every effort should be made to make decisions consistent.* Even though you're not tenuring, say, "a chemical engineer" but "Diane who happens to be a chemical engineer," care must be taken to make sure that standards are applied equitably to all candidates. To the extent that is humanly possible, it should be the case that the same decision would be reached regardless of who serves on the review committee. In particular, the AAUP warns against allowing personal characteristics—such as race, gender, disability, or national origin—to affect the decision, particularly if these classes are protected by the institution's nondiscrimination policy. (I address the matter of collegiality later in this chapter.) No matter how close a member of the committee is to an applicant, information shouldn't be shared with or leaked to one candidate that isn't provided to all candidates simultaneously. Also, to the greatest extent possible, tenure decisions should flow logically from all other evaluations made during the applicant's probationary period.

3. *Evaluations should be candid.* It doesn't help a faculty member for the evaluations made during his or her probationary period to be consistently positive in an effort to improve that person's morale, and then for the person to receive a negative tenure decision as a surprise. Similarly, the tenure evaluation process itself should be candid. Strengths should be cited in justifying positive recommendations, but weaknesses should also be noted as a stimulus to ongoing faculty development. In negative tenure decisions, institutional policy or recommendations from legal counsel may prohibit the school from giving unsuccessful applicants a reason for the denial. Nevertheless, that negative result should largely be anticipated by the faculty member because he or she heard similar concerns during his or her annual evaluation or merit review process and hasn't sufficiently addressed those areas of weakness.

4. *Unsuccessful candidates should be treated humanely.* Although candidates receiving negative tenure decisions may often not be told the reason for that result, there's no requirement that an institution turn its back on them completely. They should be treated professionally and compassionately, with assistance provided to whatever extent possible so that they can find positions elsewhere. In situations where a faculty member has a terminal year before the expiration of the contract, efforts should be taken that the person not feel any more isolated than necessary and still respected as a person and employee. (See American Council on Education, American Association of University Professors, and United Educators Insurance Risk Retention Group, 2000, and the summary provided at http://www.aaup.org/AAUP/pubsres/academe/2000/ND/NB/teneval.htm).

In addition to these four principles, several other policies ought to be regarded as best practices in how to provide both rigor and fairness when making tenure decisions. For instance, David Fite (2006) has noted that when a decision to grant or withhold tenure is challenged in court, even the most confidential aspects of the decision may become public if it is challenged in public:

In 1990 the Supreme Court ruled that university tenure reviews are not shielded by any special privilege from the general laws of evidence, which means that "confidential" views from tenure processes can be exposed to public and legal scrutiny. Another change in the law has taken employment discrimination cases out of the purview of judges and placed them in the hands of juries, who are regarded as more skeptical of institutions and sympathetic to the individual faculty member [pp. 185–186, citing Franke, 2001].

For this reason, no matter how privileged your university regulations declare the discussions of a tenure review committee to be, no comment should ever be made, even behind closed doors, that would become problematic for the committee or institution if it were to be made public. This stipulation means that you must do more than monitor your own statements made during discussions about a faculty member's tenure status; you must also remind other members of the tenure committee to focus only on the legitimate merits of the candidate's application. A comment about someone's sexual orientation or ethnicity, for example, could later be regarded as evidence of discrimination against a candidate if an appeal reaches the courts, particularly if the judgment is placed in the hands of a jury.

Fite also cautions against the practice commonly called "managing through." Committees at lower levels of the institution, such as in the department or college, will sometimes make positive recommendations about a candidate on the assumption that the really tough decisions will be made by the university committee or upper administration. This practice often leads to disaster. Just as when a faculty member receives a series of glowing annual evaluations, only to be denied tenure in his or her sixth year, managing through creates a situation that is ripe for a grievance or appeal. The faculty member can rightly claim that those who knew his or her record best were clearly in support of tenure being granted, while only those far removed from the discipline believed that the application was weak. If a negative tenure recommendation is truly warranted and the paper trail leading up to this decision has been clear, then the tough calls should be made at the lowest level possible at the institution, without an expectation that others will take a stand where the department or college did not. (See Fite, 2006, and Buller, 2008.)

In addition, tenure decisions have to be based on both the quality of the faculty member's work and the likely long-term needs of the institution. It doesn't make sense to tie up a line with a tenured faculty member if a discipline will probably be reduced or eliminated in the next five to ten years. Remember that tenure is not simply a reward for excellent service; it is also a significant financial commitment on the part of the institution. You wouldn't be a good steward of your school's resources if you committed it to an extended contract with someone whose skills and expertise will soon no longer be necessary. Finally, there's a need to consider the intangible factors too. The University of Wyoming's guide (n.d.) states,

> *Teaching, research, and service are essential, but there are intangible factors, too.* An academic department is an intellectual ecosystem, as is a university. Both require a diverse array of talents to thrive. To foster robust teaching, we must have faculty members with curricular vision, innovative teaching ideas, and the ability to serve as mentors to their younger colleagues. Strong research requires many different types of contributions: the creative spark needed to generate novel ideas, the talent to render these ideas compelling to one's peers, the ability to organize and lead teams of people having various disciplinary backgrounds and skills, the entrepreneurial skills needed to secure necessary resources. Effective service requires strong interpersonal skills, collegiality, and, occasionally, sheer physical stamina to get things done [p. 3].

○ the role of collegiality in tenure decisions

One of the most difficult of intangible factors for most reviewers to address is the collegiality of a faculty member. While some institutions regard collegiality as a separate criterion for tenure (along with teaching, research, and service) and others treat it as a subcategory under their standards for teaching or service, most policy manuals on tenure decisions don't address this issue at all. That situation leaves many reviewers in a dilemma: Do I ignore a severe lack of collegiality in making this tenure decision because our policy doesn't address it, or do I avoid the possible damage that can be done to the discipline and institution by hiring such an uncollegial faculty member?

In addressing this problem, it's important to recognize that in the United States at least, there's no legal barrier to considering a faculty member's collegiality when making tenure decisions. In the case of *Mayberry v. Dees* (1981), for instance, the Fourth Circuit Court established that collegiality was a valid criterion in tenure decisions alongside such widely accepted criteria as teaching, scholarship, and service. Moreover, in the case of the *University of Baltimore v. Iz* (1998), the Maryland Appellate Court ruled that collegiality may be considered when personnel decisions are being made, even if an institution's governance documents do not expressly cite collegiality as a distinct criterion. (On the history of collegiality issues, see Cipriano, 2011; Connell, 2001; Connell and Savage, 2001; and Fogg, 2002.)

Nevertheless, although it's possible to use collegiality as a criterion when making tenure decisions, it can be extremely challenging to document the presence or absence of this quality in an effective manner. For teaching, research, and service, there are quantifiable and measurable factors that can be considered, such as the number of peer-reviewed articles, scores on student and peer teaching evaluations, and length of committee service. In addition, qualitative evaluation of progress in these areas can also be determined through the types of portfolios that we'll consider in Chapter Eleven. But as of yet, no similar mechanism exists for the systematic measurement or evaluation of collegiality.

If lack of collegiality is truly an issue in a tenure decision, you'll need to provide documentation of some sort. Firsthand written accounts of recognizably unprofessional behavior, particularly those that were detrimental to the institutional missions of teaching, scholarship, and service, are especially useful. Secondhand accounts ("Well, I heard that . . . ") or anonymous reports are of little value. It's necessary to have documentation of instances where the faculty member impeded the fundamental work of the institution, perhaps through behavior that made it impossible for a committee to do its job or a refusal to accept commonly assigned tasks.

Remember that the time to start preparing for a faculty member's evaluation isn't a month or two before your recommendation is due but the day that person begins work or has completed his or her last evaluation. Just as you should keep good personal records of achievements or problems that have arisen in the faculty member's instruction, research, and service, so should you record in your notes specific examples of great success or challenges a person has had in promoting an atmosphere of collegiality and professionalism. In other words, in order for collegiality to be a legitimate factor in a tenure decision, it's not enough to argue that someone was curmudgeonly or occasionally unsocial. The real question to ask in all such cases is: What documentable harm was done by the person's behavior? (See Arreola, 2007.) Then be sure to retain those notes at least as long as is required by your institution's policy on the retention of documents and any applicable laws. Your institution's legal counsel or internal auditor is likely to be a valuable resource for the nature and extent of those requirements.

○ how to convey the results of a negative tenure evaluation

While it's always difficult to convey bad news to a faculty member, it's particularly trying to tell someone that he or she will not receive tenure. No matter how you attempt to sugarcoat that information, you are informing the person that he or she will soon no longer have a job and, in fact, may have difficulty remaining within his or her chosen career. After all, university search committees are often leery of candidates who are applying after six or seven years in a tenure-track position. Particularly when the job market is not good, they may decide to focus on candidates who don't appear to have failed at another institution. The most important thing to keep in mind when telling someone that he or she has been denied tenure is to be direct but humane.

Start, as always, by following your institution's procedure to the letter. If you're permitted to do so, have a witness present who can attest that you adhered to the established process should there ever be a question. In most cases, this witness should be someone from human resources, legal affairs, or the office of the dean or provost who can guide you in the procedures and has probably had a lot more experience in these situations than you have. Tell the unsuccessful applicant what you're required to say, looking the faculty member in the eye and adopting a demeanor that's neither dismissive, threatening, nor condescending. Don't say anything beyond what you're required to say and have decided to say before the meeting began. Understand that the person may be upset or angry at this news, or that these emotions may arise later once he or she has had a chance to process the impact of this decision. As in so many other cases when you're conveying bad news, the faculty member may react very little at that moment but is likely to follow up later with a number of questions and concerns. Expect that this type of confrontation will occur at some point, and try not to be blindsided if it occurs when you are walking across campus, at a community event, or relaxing at home. Remember that once you've had your initial meeting, these follow-up questions could arrive at any time. (See Buller, 2012.)

Oral notification of a negative tenure result should always be accompanied or followed by written notification. At many institutions, this letter is conveyed to the faculty member as part of the initial meeting. (One advantage of having a witness present is that he or she can verify that this written notification was duly delivered.) But it would be unnecessarily heartless for a faculty member to learn of a negative tenure decision solely from a memo, letter, or e-mail. Good news can be conveyed by any medium; bad news should be conveyed face-to-face whenever possible. The subtext of this meeting should be, "You're still a good person. You have many fine skills and talents. At the present time, unfortunately, you and the institution were not a good long-term match" (American Council on Education, American Association of University Professors, and United Educators Insurance Risk Retention Group, 2000).

You can be generous in allowing the faculty member to use some of the institution's resources and facilities to find a new position. Even if your travel funding is specifically set aside for faculty development, it may be wise to allocate some travel funding to the unsuccessful tenure candidate so that he or she can network at a conference with institutions that have vacancies. In a similar way, permitting the person to use the institution's photocopying and videoconferencing resources as part of a job search can be a gracious and compassionate way to soften the blow that this decision inevitably has.

mini-case studies: tenure evaluations

You are evaluating a candidate for tenure whose student course evaluations are at the median for his or her department. Peer evaluations of teaching suggest that there are some hurdles to overcome in the candidate's effectiveness, although as the official report states, "notable improvement has occurred during the past year." The candidate has published four articles of research in journals that are peer-reviewed and somewhat respected in his or her discipline, but they are not considered to be among the first-tier publications in the field. The candidate has been a member of one committee for three of his or her six years at the institution, and this committee is regarded as one of the school's most important and challenging service opportunities.

Based solely on what you know so far, try to determine whether this candidate is likely to be successful or unsuccessful in applying for tenure at your institution and in your discipline. If you believe that the candidate would be unsuccessful, what about this person's portfolio would be regarded as inadequate?

o o o

You are meeting with a candidate who has been denied tenure at the institution. The purpose of this meeting is to inform the candidate of this result. An associate provost has joined you at this meeting to provide guidance and serve as a witness. Try to determine how you believe you would react and what you might say in each of the following circumstances:

- The candidate breaks into tears and sobs uncontrollably.
- The candidate gets angry and shouts at you.
- The candidate gets angry and threatens you.
- The candidate says something that leads you to believe he or she may harm himself or herself.
- The candidate says something that leads you to believe he or she may harm those responsible for this decision.

o o o

A faculty member in your area is a member of a protected class. Ever since this person's first day on the job, she has called herself "a lawsuit just waiting to happen" and said things like, "I've been treated unfairly by schools before, and that will not happen here." Over the course of the past six years, this faculty member has had a difficult relationship with others at the institution. When she comes up for tenure, her qualifications are on the borderline of acceptability. The critical factor, however, has been the number of faculty members who wrote the tenure committee in confidence to say that due to the candidate's lack of collegiality, they were adamantly opposed to granting her tenure. Your institution does not regard collegiality as a separate criterion for tenure and, in fact, the word collegiality never appears in your institution's bylaws and policies.

Although you have mixed feelings yourself, the institution's promotion and tenure committee has voted against tenuring this faculty member. Your own supervisor supports this decision. You are asked to meet with the faculty member and convey the results of the tenure process. What special steps or precautions might you take in this situation? How might you break the news to the faculty member?

○ conclusion

The stakes riding on an institution's tenure decision are extremely high for the school and the candidate. For the school, tenure reflects a substantial long-term investment. If you make the wrong decision, you're either losing someone who could have been of incredible value to the discipline or committing the institution to a relationship that's not a good use of its energy and resources. For the candidate, tenure can be the key to either a long and rewarding career or, if denied, a possible lifetime of temporary positions, part-time positions, or work far from the person's area of specialty. For these reasons, tenure decisions should always be made with great care, their results conveyed with great compassion, and the policies behind them carefully designed to promote both rigor and equity.

References

Amacher, R. C., & Meiners, R. E. (2004). *Faulty towers: Tenure and the structure of higher education*. Oakland, CA: Independent Institute.

American Council on Education, American Association of University Professors, & United Educators Insurance Risk Retention Group. (2000). *Good practice in tenure evaluation: Advice for tenured faculty, department chairs, and academic administrators*. Washington, DC: American Council on Education. Retrieved from http://www.acenet.edu/bookstore/pdf/tenure-evaluation.pdf.

American Association of University Professors. (1915). *1915 declaration of principles on academic freedom and academic tenure*. Retrieved from http://www.aaup.org/AAUP/pubsres/policydocs/contents/1915.htm.

Arreola, R. A. (2007). *Developing a comprehensive faculty evaluation system: A guide to designing, building, and operating large-scale faculty evaluation systems*. San Francisco: Jossey-Bass/Anker.

Buller, J. L. (2008). The "Spider-Man principle" and the "categorical imperative": How to address the problem of "managing through." *Academic Leader, 24*(4), 2–3.

Buller, J. L. (2012). *The essential department chair: A comprehensive desk reference* (2nd ed.). San Francisco: Jossey-Bass.

Church of England. (2004). *The book of common prayer and administration of the sacraments and other rites and ceremonies of the Church according to the use of the Church of England*. Cambridge: Cambridge University Press.

Cipriano, R. E. (2011). *Facilitating a collegial department in higher education: Strategies for success*. San Francisco: Jossey-Bass.

Connell, M. A. (2001). The role of collegiality in higher education tenure, promotion, and termination decisions. *Journal of College and University Law, 27*, 833–858.

Connell, M. A., & Savage, F. G. (2001). Does collegiality count? *Academe, 87*(6), 37–41.

Dooris, M. J. (2002). Institutional research to enhance faculty performance. In C. L. Colbeck (Ed.), *Evaluating faculty performance*. San Francisco: Jossey-Bass.

Fite, D. (2006). Using evaluation data for personnel decisions. In P. Seldin (Ed.), *Evaluating faculty performance: A practical guide to assessing teaching, research, and service*. San Francisco: Jossey-Bass/Anker.

Fogg, P. (2002, April 26). Nevada Supreme Court rules against professor who was denied tenure. *Chronicle of Higher Education*, A14.

Franke, A. (2001). Making defensible tenure decisions. *Academe, 87*(6), 32–36.

Jimenez v. Almodovar. (1981). 650 F.2d 363 (1st Cir.).

Kaplin, W. A., & Lee, B. A. (2006). *The law of higher education: A comprehensive guide to legal implications of administrative decision making*. San Francisco: Jossey-Bass.

Krotkoff v. Goucher College. (1978). 585 F.2d 675 (4th Cir.).

Loope, D. R. (1995). *Academic tenure: Its origins, administration, and importance*. Columbia: South Carolina Commission on Higher Education.

Mayberry v. Dees. (1981). 663 F.2d 502 (4th Cir. Ct.).

Stripling, J. (2011, May 15). Most presidents prefer no tenure for majority of faculty. *Chronicle of Higher Education*. Retrieved from http://chronicle.com/article/Most-Presidents-Favor-No/127526/.

Rosovsky, H. (1991). *The university: An owner's manual*. New York: Norton.

Shannahan, J. (1973). A brief history of tenure. *Clearing House, 47*, 276.

Silber, J. (1989). *Straight shooting: What's wrong with America and how to fix it*. New York: HarperCollins.

Snyder, M. (2000). Tenure in perspective. *Academe, 86*, 103.

Trower, C. (2000). The trouble with tenure. *National Forum, 79*(1), 24–29.

University of Wyoming. (n.d.). *Making tenure decisions: Philosophy, criteria, and expectations*. Laramie, WY: UWYO Office of Academic Affairs. Retrieved from http://www.uwyo.edu/acadaffairs/_files/docs/Tenure_phil_criteria_expect.pdf.

University of Baltimore v. Iz. (1998). 716 A.2d 1107 (Md. Ct. App.).

Resources

Buller, J. L. (2007) Improving documentation for promotion and tenure. *Academic Leader, 23*(11), 8–9.

Commission on Academic Tenure in Higher Education, Keast, W. R., & Macy, J. W. (1973). *Faculty tenure: A report and recommendations.* San Francisco: Jossey-Bass.

Few, A. L., Piercy, F. P., & Stremmel, A. J. (2007). Balancing the passion for activism with the demands of tenure: One professional's story from three perspectives. *NWSA Journal, 19*(3), 47–66.

Miller, R. I. (1987). *Evaluating faculty for promotion and tenure.* San Francisco: Jossey-Bass.

9

promotion evaluations

In Chapter Eight, we saw three reasons why promotion decisions are different from tenure decisions:

1. Promotion rewards a faculty member for what he or she has accomplished in the past; tenure decisions focus on what an institution expects a faculty member to achieve in the future.
2. Promotion is usually "transportable" in a way that tenure isn't. When faculty members move from institution to institution, they almost always retain their rank but only sometimes retain their tenure status.
3. Being turned down for promotion means being told, "Not now," by an institution; the candidate can almost always reapply in the future. Being turned down for tenure means being told, "Not at all"; a negative tenure decision usually leads to a terminal contract.

To these three differences, we may now add a fourth: going up for tenure is usually an activity that, if the applicant is successful, a faculty member does only once per institution; going up for promotion is an activity that even if the applicant is successful, often occurs at least twice at an institution. Because of these differences, it's useful to examine promotion evaluations separately from tenure considerations, even

173

though most (though certainly not all) institutions tend to combine the granting of tenure and promotion to the rank of associate professor into a single process.

○ aligning promotion evaluations with institutional, national, and international standards

The first task reviewers should perform when considering the credentials of an applicant for promotion is to ask, "How well does this faculty member's achievements stack up against those who previously were promoted to this rank in this discipline at this institution?" To break this question down into its component parts:

1. Does the candidate meet the standards for this rank established by his or her department?
2. Does the candidate meet the standards for this rank established by his or her college or division?
3. Does the candidate meet the standards for this rank established by the institution?
4. Are the candidate's achievements at all comparable to others who have been promoted at this institution to this rank in this discipline during the recent past?

It's important to consider all these questions regardless of the level at which you're reviewing the candidate. For example, if you're conducting a departmental promotion review, it does you very little good to recommend a candidate who can't meet the requirements at the next two levels. Similarly, at the university level, it's not advisable to make a practice of overturning departmental decisions based on that discipline's stringent requirements simply because expectations institution-wide are looser or more flexible. Certainly there are times when members of a departmental review committee have tried to impose standards that are unrealistic and largely unattainable, but these situations are best addressed at the policy level rather than on a case-by-case basis. What's more common is that the people who are most familiar with the discipline understand the standards that pertain to their field at comparable institutions and so have developed requirements that are more demanding than those of the college or university. So if you ignore the discipline's own perspective on this issue, you may be placing that department in a situation where its reputation will suffer among its peers or its accreditation status may come to be in jeopardy.

Determining whether the candidate's credentials are comparable to those of earlier successful applicants is also an important way for you as a reviewer to pursue both rigor and equity. There may well be circumstances that lead a college or university to raise its standards for faculty work, perhaps because its mission is evolving or it's seeking to become more selective. In these cases, an application for promotion that would've been successful ten or fifteen years ago may not be successful today. But if these changes are occurring, the institution needs to inform faculty members well in advance, giving them time to meet the new requirements or to delay applying for promotion. Such a change shouldn't come as a surprise when an actual application is being considered. Moreover, institutions should raise standards in a careful and meaningful manner. The two-year regional teaching college that attempts to impose criteria more appropriate for a flagship research university isn't serving the best interests of either its students or its faculty members. What may be occurring is that faculty members who have already been promoted have been tempted to adopt standards that they themselves couldn't have met when they went up for review or that reflect their levels of achievement now rather than a few decades in the past. As a reviewer, you have an important role to play by asking, "Is this portfolio similar in quality to those that were successful in the past? If it is but there's still resistance to approving it, is there a legitimate reason for that resistance?"

As we've seen, although you have to be aware of standards that are appropriate for the institution itself, you can't ignore national and international expectations entirely. Institutional reputations suffer when it becomes clear that their associate and full professors are significantly less accomplished than those holding these ranks at peer institutions. In general, the following definitions of ranks apply to most colleges and universities when decisions about rank are made in the United States:

- *Assistant professor:* An entry-level faculty position for candidates holding the terminal degree or a terminal promotion from the rank of instructor for those who lack the terminal degree but have demonstrated consistent and sustained excellence in teaching, scholarship, and service.
- *Associate professor:* A senior rank typically requiring at least six years of full-time service as a faculty member at a college or university. Associate professors should have demonstrated excellence in teaching, substantial achievement in scholarship or creative activity as determined by their peers, and a commitment to serving the department, discipline, institution, or community.
- *Professor:* The highest faculty rank bestowed on those who have met and exceeded all criteria for promotion to the rank of associate professor, held that senior rank for an appropriate length of time, and achieved distinction in the profession. Professors should have demonstrated consistent excellence in teaching, achievements in scholarship or creative activity that are regarded as significant beyond the institution itself, and a level of service befitting a high-ranking member of the academic community.

But even within these widely accepted definitions, there's still a great deal of room for institutional priorities. For example, at Boston University, the "substantial achievement in scholarship" required of associate professors is defined as enjoying "a national reputation as a scholar or professional" (http://www.bu.edu/handbook/appointments-and-promotions/classification-of-ranks-and-titles/), while the Community and Technical College at the University of Alaska Anchorage defines an associate professor as someone whose expertise in research "is recognized within the community, region, and state" (http://www.uaa.alaska.edu/ctc/forms/upload/PromotionTenure.pdf). Similarly, the level of research expected of full professors at the University of Florida includes "evidence of more extensive productivity in the area of scholarly activity [than associate professors], documented by [such indications as] . . . [a r]ecord of continued publication of original articles in quality peer-reviewed scientific journals as first or senior author [or a s]ignificant track record of continued research productivity supported by peer-reviewed external funding and/or significant contracts or services." At Volunteer State Community College in Tennessee, the research expectation for promotion to the rank of professor is defined as "documented evidence of sustained high quality professional productivity in . . . scholarship/creative activities/research" (http://www.volstate.edu/Documents/FacultyHandbook.pdf). In other words, although teaching institutions are likely to place more emphasis on the quality of instruction and research institutions are likely to place more emphasis on the quality of scholarship, a consensus has emerged that achievements in these areas should be significant for associate professors and substantial and ongoing for full professors. Most important, promotion decisions should never be based on seniority alone. Regardless of the mission of the institution, colleges and universities that promote people simply "because it's time" or because "she's paid her dues" devalue the coinage of rank in higher education generally. They reduce rather than enhance the likelihood that the titles of their senior faculty members will be respected elsewhere.

○ best practices in promotion evaluations

Since promotion evaluations directly affect the careers and livelihood of faculty members, many institutions are continually refining their procedures to make them as effective and fair as possible. The following are among the best practices currently in use at many colleges and universities.

Evaluators should be of equal or higher rank to the rank being considered for promotion

It's difficult to know precisely what it takes to be a professor or associate professor if you haven't reached that rank yourself. For this reason, most institutions limit the committees reviewing applicants for the highest rank to those who are already full professors. In a similar way, committees reviewing applicants for the rank of associate professor are usually restricted to current associate and full professors. This policy has an added advantage of helping to promote collegiality since the committee is essentially welcoming successful applicants into their own ranks. In addition, it reduces the likelihood of log-rolling: assistant professors who vote in favor of others since they know that those individuals will someday be voting on them.

External letters of review are useful, but far less so when reviewers are selected by the faculty member alone

Since promotion has a meaning that spans institutions, external letters of review can provide an objective analysis of whether the accomplishments of the individual truly merit the proposed rank. Nevertheless, it's a poor practice to allow the applicants to choose their own external reviewers. Almost everyone in academia has three to five close friends at other institutions who are willing to write a letter of support. Members of the review committee should thus use their own networks in order to identify individuals who can be completely impartial in reviewing the qualifications of the applicant.

Minority opinions should be expressed, without attribution, when the report is forwarded to the next level of review

Since promotion decisions are almost always made in a multitiered manner—the departmental committee recommending to the college or division, which then recommends to an institutional committee—it's important for each level of that procedure to have a clear understanding of the previous group's rationale. If a committee of fifteen simply submits a positive recommendation for a candidate, it's impossible to tell whether that recommendation was unanimous or based on a vote of eight to seven. Supplying numerical votes, as well as an anonymous summary of the minority's argument, helps higher-level committees better understand the full picture of a candidate's application and directs their attention to key issues.

Evidence of teaching effectiveness should be made in a variety of ways, not based on student course evaluations alone
Student evaluations can reveal much of importance. They can tell you whether the professor speaks clearly in class, distributes a syllabus early in the term, adheres to the policies set forth in that syllabus, returns assignments in a timely manner, and is readily available outside class. Everyone knows that there will always be students who get these matters wrong. For instance, some students will claim that the course didn't have a syllabus when it did, or that the professor never kept his or her office hours when he or she was readily available. But reviewers quickly learn to dismiss remarks that run counter to the overall pattern, and student course evaluations usually exist in numbers large enough for clear patterns to emerge. But students can't tell you everything. They're not in a position to know whether the professor has remained current in his or her field, has adopted pedagogical techniques appropriate for the discipline, has included suitable material in organizing the course, has chosen a textbook that's up to date, and has properly paced the course to increase the likelihood of effective learning. These matters are best determined by those who are themselves experts in the discipline, and those experts are to be found among the applicant's faculty peers. In certain instances, however, even peer evaluations don't go far enough:

> Especially when the teaching career spans many years, student course evaluations and peer observation reports should be supplemented by evidence of professional accomplishments by former students, the impact of the candidate's teaching innovations on this campus or elsewhere, the candidate's influence on educational practices or

policies on a regional or national scale, or other contributions out-side the classroom, as appropriate [University of North Carolina at Greensboro, 2006].

The goal must always be to identify sources that can best help the review committee discover whatever it needs to know.

The group conducting a peer review should always include observers who have no close connection to the faculty member being evaluated

As one report notes,

> The reliability of evaluators is also shaped by the nature of their rela-tionships with the person being evaluated. A 2000 study shows that when teachers are allowed to choose their own evaluators, those eval-uators produce assessments that are at considerable variance with assessments from other colleagues or administrators. . . . A different sort of problem based on social relationships emerges when evalua-tors judge colleagues purely on the basis of reputation, in the form of impressions gleaned from "faculty lounge discussions," "debates at department meetings," conversations with students, and "quadrangle discussion" [Iowa State University, 1995–2011, citing Centra, 2000, and Kulik and Ericksen, 1974].

For this reason, peer evaluators, like the sources of external letters of support, should be carefully selected by the review group itself rather than by the candidate who is up for promotion.

All reviewers should be aware that because the nature of scholarship is so varied, promotion applications may reflect nontraditional patterns in such areas as the subject of the faculty member's research, his or her rates of productivity, and even the discipline itself

What research means today is far more complex than it was twenty or thirty years ago. In addition to Ernest Boyer's (1990) famous division of scholarship into four categories—discovery, integration, application, and teaching—promotion committees will also encounter scholarship that seems not to fit into traditional pigeonholes or is published only electronically and virtually.

Reviewers need to be aware that valid professional research now occurs in many forms, and some of these forms may not have existed when the members were first developing their own research agendas. Robert Diamond (2004) provides some good examples of how to explain the significance of nontraditional forms of scholarship to those who may not be familiar with these research methods. In addition, many universities are far more sensitive today to the rhythms of life than they were in the past. They recognize that productivity may rise and fall as faculty members raise their families, take care of aging parents, or deal with any of the other challenges that can complicate people's lives. Here's how this type of flexibility is described by the University of Alaska Fairbanks (n.d.):

> Strong narratives typically demonstrate the coherent themes in the candidate's work and effectively explain and contextualize accomplishments and contributions. If a candidate's profile might be considered atypical, it is especially important to provide a context for understanding the contributions [p. 16].

In most cases, the candidate or the candidate's department will provide that context, but if this doesn't occur, the review committee itself should be willing to investigate these circumstances.

In multilevel promotion reviews, the candidate should be informed of the result at each level and, if applicable, given a chance to improve sections of the portfolio about which there were questions

As we've seen, there are typically several stages to a promotion application. If the candidate isn't informed of the result at each level, he or she may assume that an unsuccessful application was blocked only at an upper level where he or she is less well known and people seem remote from the applicant's discipline; the applicant may not be aware that there were consistently negative votes at each stage of the process and thus misunderstand the reasons for the decision. Moreover, in cases where there's a negative recommendation at a lower level or the recommendation is positive but some questions or reservations have arisen, alerting the candidate to what has occurred and allowing the portfolio to be improved is of benefit to everyone. It may well be that an area attracting concern wasn't documented in an effective manner or that the cover letter was vague or misleading. When an applicant is able to address these issues early in the process, the work of reviewers at the upper levels is easier as well as more equitable. And "if applicants receive feedback at each level of the review, campus policies should exist regarding the nature of the message (for example, specific strengths and weaknesses, rationale for decisions)" (Braskamp and Ory, 1994, p. 161).

In addition, it serves very little purpose for institutions to declare a promotion portfolio locked once it's been submitted and to prevent candidates from adding new publications, grants, or awards that have occurred in the interim. A promotion application should consider the entirety of a candidate's record, with particular attention to his or her achievements at that institution and since any prior promotion. Since recent evidence of positive achievements is part of that record, there's no reason to exclude it.

○ benefiting from best practices regardless of your current procedures

Since a number of these best practices deal more with institutional policy than with the practice of individual reviewers, what can you gain from them if your system handles promotions in a different way?

For one thing, you now have an excellent opportunity to demonstrate academic leadership by proposing that your school consider adopting the policies that have proven effective at other schools. Second, you can adapt several features of them to your own strategies in reviewing applications for promotion. For instance, you can ask for permission to obtain external review letters even if your institution doesn't ordinarily do so or has applicants secure their own letters of support. You can take the initiative to learn about a faculty member's teaching from more sources than student course evaluations alone. You can ask to sit in on a few classes, review course syllabi and exams, and learn what you can about the success of students whom the faculty member has mentored. You can learn as much as possible about acceptable forms of scholarship in that person's field if it's not the same as yours. You can try to determine the appropriate level of research productivity for successful promotion candidates in that field at comparable institutions. And you can begin viewing the person's record as a pattern, not a set of isolated achievements. For instance, does the quality of instruction seem to be getting better or worse? Is research productivity increasing? If scholarship seems sporadic, are there factors related to that person's research focus or personal life that may be responsible? In other words, unless your institution's policies explicitly forbid reviewers from engaging in some of these best practices, ask your supervisor about whether any of them are possible. You'll end up developing a clearer picture of the candidate's achievements, and you may cause your institution to improve its policies as a result.

Promoting Faculty Members to the Rank of Professor

Evaluations that deal with promotion to the rank of full professor present their own set of opportunities and challenges. Many institutional policies dealing with promotion to the rank of associate professor are rather detailed. They may even specify the number of publications the faculty member needs to have, the amount of required grant activity, minimum acceptable scores on student ratings of instruction or peer reviews, or some other objective standard. These specific requirements are far less common in the case of reviews leading to the rank of professor. These guidelines are often quite general and don't provide the reviewer with a great deal of guidance. For instance, at West Virginia University, the requirements specify the minimum number of years the applicant has to have served as associate professor (in this case, five), but other criteria are described as simply being at a higher level than that expected of associate professors:

> Promotion to the rank of full professor is the highest academic honor that the University awards to its own faculty. Clearly, standards for achievement and performance must be much higher for the promotion to full professor than to associate professor. The candidate must substantially have exceeded the minimum contributions required for the rank of associate professor. . . . [In the area of teaching, the candidate must demonstrate] continued adherence to the standards required for promotion to associate professor for the entire period since the previous promotion or the time of joining the University. . . . The candidate for promotion to full professor will have become a mature and productive scholar within at least one sub-field of the faculty member's academic discipline. Evidence will include publications in refereed journals of high quality with secondary importance attached to other outlets for scholarly research. Research and refereed publications will count heavily in the promotion to professor. A steady level of research activity is also important. . . . [In the area of service,] the candidate must demonstrate a strong leadership role in the College, University, or external community [www.be.wvu.edu/faculty_staff/resources_downloads/criteria_ promotion_tenure.doc].

These requirements are fairly typical of the way in which most institutions describe their criteria. They provide the review committee with an admirable degree of flexibility in adapting the criteria to the different forms in which excellent teaching, research, and service are demonstrated in different disciplines. But they don't give reviewers a clear standard by which to know how much productivity in each of these areas is sufficient. For this reason, review committees should have a discussion, before they begin considering individual cases, of what they'll be looking for in the portfolios. Past precedent has to be considered: if twelve peer-reviewed articles were acceptable last year, requiring candidates to have thirty this year is excessive—but, like everything else, these can adapt gradually to an institution's evolving mission and profile. The important thing is to be consistent among candidates this year and to be consistent—to a reasonable extent but also accounting for institutional change—with successful candidates in the past.

Another factor that makes promotion to the rank of professor different from other types of review is that institutions vary widely in terms of when faculty members typically submit materials for this process. Although most colleges and universities require faculty members to wait at least five years after receiving the rank of associate professor to go up for full professor, custom and tradition take over at this point. At some institutions, almost everyone applies for promotion once that fifth year has arrived, and it's considered to be a sign of failure not to be promoted at the earliest possible opportunity. At others, almost no one is considered for promotion as soon as he or she becomes eligible, and it's considered to be a sign of great distinction to be promoted in such a short time.

As a reviewer, you'll need to be aware of local practice in this regard because it'll help determine how much achievement since the faculty member's last promotion your school is probably looking for. If it tends to promote people quickly, another book, grant, or handful of articles, accompanied by evidence of effective teaching, may be all that's required. If people customarily don't become full professors until they've served at the associate rank for eight or more years, a much more compelling case may be necessary.

Although it's not something that you can control, you should be aware that institutions with a reputation for promoting everyone to full professor extremely early, when many applicants are still in their early to mid-thirties, develop a reputation over time for not maintaining exceptionally high standards. Since you want your own promotion and those of your colleagues to mean something significant across academia, you may wish to urge decision makers at your institution to begin raising the bar for promotion to full professor so that in time, it becomes the true distinction it was intended to be.

Evaluating Faculty Members for Special Ranks

Even if schools tend not to promote faculty members quickly, it's possible to hold the rank of full professor for twenty or more years. During that time, the vast majority of faculty members have no opportunity at all for another promotion. For this reason, institutions sometimes develop special ranks that give people the chance to be granted a distinction that rises above the rank of professor.

Named chairs are perhaps the most common of these "superranks," but chaired positions typically require large endowments that help fund part of the individual's salary. Other titles—such as research professor, eminent scholar, distinguished teaching professor, and integrated scholar—may be created by the institution to recognize exceptional achievements by highly meritorious individuals. At times, professors must apply for these titles, just as they'd apply for any other promotion; at other times, these distinctions are simply awarded by the institution as an honor (and occasionally as a surprise) to the people receiving them. In either case, however, if you're asked to review candidates for one of these titles, it's important to preserve the integrity of what should be a highly prestigious and rare honor. Take special care to resist the pressure some people may exert to grant a distinguished title to someone merely because that person has been a fixture at the institution for a long time. In order for these titles to remain true honors, the standards for granting them should be exceptionally high. Ask yourself and other members of the review community whether the candidate has genuinely performed at a level rarely achieved at your institution or has simply amassed a record typical for someone whose career in higher education has spanned several decades. There may, of course, be situations where it's advisable to grant one of these titles to a sentimental favorite, such as a dearly beloved faculty member who has been diagnosed with a terminal illness, but their value will be lost if they become perceived as an entitlement based only on seniority.

mini-case studies: promotion evaluations

You're chair of a promotion review committee that's considering the application of a faculty member who's up for promotion to the rank of professor. This faculty member has applied for promotion in the minimum allowable amount of time since becoming an associate professor. In that interim, the faculty member has been ranked by both peers and students as "very good" in teaching (the second of five ranks, appearing just below "exceptional"), has written five more refereed research articles (two in first-tier journals, three in second-tier journals), received a small external grant for forty-eight thousand dollars, and has served as a member of the faculty senate every year since the previous promotion. Colleagues in the department and college report that this faculty member is "collegial but somewhat reserved."

All other factors being equal, would this candidate qualify for promotion to the rank of professor at your institution? If so, are there particular achievements of this faculty member you can point to that clearly take this application over the bar? If not, what would the faculty member need to do in order to have a successful application next time?

o o o

Your institution is considering a new policy requiring unsuccessful applicants for promotion to the rank of full professor to wait at least three years before applying again. The rationale given by advocates for this new policy is that the rank of professor is so eminent that a truly significant record of achievement is required, and unsuccessful applicants cannot meet those stringent requirements in only one year. The supporters of the new plan have observed that the same unsuccessful candidates keep applying year after year, with the result that the low morale of these candidates is affecting others at the institution, the committee wastes a great deal of time debating the same cases each year, and the president wants promotion standards to increase in order to raise the profile of the institution. As a result, candidates who didn't qualify under the old criteria will need additional time to become eligible under the new, tougher criteria.

Would you support such a policy? Why or why not?

(Continued)

o   o   o

Your institution currently links the granting of tenure with promotion to the rank of associate professor: candidates can't receive one without receiving the other. The result has been that a number of excellent candidates, who surely would have qualified if they had an additional two or three years have been given terminal contracts because they didn't quite meet all the requirements in their sixth year of full-time teaching. A new policy has been proposed that would de-couple promotion and tenure decisions. Advocates for this new policy argue that the institution has lost a number of truly superb teachers and mentors due to its policy of linking tenure with promotion. Valued colleagues, they suggest, could be tenured in order to retain them and then qualify for promotion to associate professor after a few years, if the two decisions were separate processes.

Would you support such a policy? Why or why not?

o   o   o

One of your responsibilities as chair of the promotion review committee is to inform unsuccessful applicants of the institution's decision. This year a member of one of your institution's protected classes unsuccessfully applied for tenure and promotion to the rank of associate professor. Failing to be granted tenure, the faculty member will now be placed on a one-year terminal contract. The committee was divided on this issue, voting eight against with six in favor of granting tenure and promotion. The upper administration and governing board have refused to overturn the committee's decision. You know this faculty member quite well, and you're aware that the person has a hot temper and is extremely litigious, having filed lawsuits against the institution several times in the past five years.

What steps would you take to prepare for the meeting in which you'd inform the candidate of the institution's decision? In the meeting itself, how would you proceed, and what would you say?

○ conclusion

Promotion decisions immediately affect a faculty member's status and, in most cases, his or her income. In addition, the majority of faculty members are considered for promotion at least twice during their careers. These factors make promotion reviews different in kind from other evaluations. In certain cases, you'll be involved in a summative process that evolves into a formative process as you assist unsuccessful applicants in understanding how they might do better next time. For this reason, promotion evaluations call for a combination of wisdom, diplomacy, and all the other skills you've developed throughout your experience in higher education.

References

Boyer E. L. (1990). *Scholarship reconsidered: Priorities of the professoriate.* Princeton, NJ: Carnegie Foundation for the Advancement of Teaching.

Braskamp, L. A., & Ory, J. C. (1994). *Assessing faculty work: Enhancing individual and institutional performance.* San Francisco: Jossey-Bass.

Centra, J. A. (2000). Evaluating the teaching portfolio: A role for colleagues. *New Directions for Teaching and Learning, 83,* 87–93.

Diamond, R. M. (2004). *Preparing for promotion, tenure, and annual review: A faculty guide* (2nd ed.). San Francisco: Jossey-Bass/Anker.

Iowa State University. Center for Excellence in Learning and Teaching. (1995–2011). *Summative peer evaluation of teaching: Literature review and best practices.* Retrieved from www.celt.iastate.edu/pet/homepage.html.

Kulik, J. A., & Ericksen, S. C. (1974, February). *Evaluation of teaching: Memo to the faculty* (Memo No. 53). Ann Arbor: Center for Research on Learning and Teaching, University of Michigan,

University of Alaska Fairbanks. (n.d.). *Best practices for promotion and tenure.* Retrieved from http://www.uaf.edu/files/provost/promotion-tenure/promotion-tenure-unac/Best_Practices.pdf.

University of North Carolina at Greensboro. College of Arts and Sciences. (2006). *Best practices in tenure and promotion.* Retrieved from www.uncg.edu/aas/deptheads/documents/BestPractices2006.doc.

Resources

Buller, J. L. (2007). Improving documentation for promotion and tenure. *Academic Leader, 23*(11), 8–9.

Youn, T. I. K., & Price, T. M. (2009) Learning from the experience of others: The evolution of faculty tenure and promotion rules in comprehensive institutions. *Journal of Higher Education, 80*(2), 204–237.

part four

quantitative and qualitative approaches to review and evaluation

10

the arreola model

At various points in this book, I've addressed both quantitative and qualitative approaches to faculty evaluation. For this reason, it seems appropriate to conclude with a deeper look at these two approaches, exploring them in the context of two major evaluative systems and then considering how these approaches might be combined. In 1995, Raoul Arreola's *Developing a Comprehensive Faculty Evaluation System*, outlining a significant new approach to the academic review process, was published. Arreola, of the University of Tennessee Health Science Center, had created this system with his colleague, Lawrence Aleamoni, of the University of Arizona. That model of evaluation was refined and expanded through two more editions of the work, culminating in the third edition that appeared in 2007. The central feature of what we might now call the Arreola model is an eight-step process that aims to be as comprehensive and objective as possible in its approach to faculty review.

1. *Determine the faculty role model.* Define what it is that faculty members do at your institution in terms of their most basic responsibilities.

2. *Determine the faculty role model parameter values.* Set priorities and weights to those various responsibilities.
3. *Define the roles in the faculty role model.* Within each responsibility, identify observable and measurable behaviors that can be used in an evaluation.
4. *Determine role component weights.* Set priorities and weights for those observable behaviors.
5. *Determine appropriate sources of information.* Identify the means by which you'll observe and measure those behaviors.
6. *Determine information source weights.* Set priorities and weights for those sources of information.
7. *Determine how information should be gathered.* Establish a procedure for obtaining the information from each source.
8. *Complete the system.* Gather the information, analyze it, and report the results to the faculty member and any other relevant offices at the institution.

The Arreola model thus doesn't provide a specific mechanism for reviewing faculty members or urge that best practices in place at one college or university be replicated at other institutions. Rather it lays out a process by which each institution can develop its own mechanism and set of criteria that suit its individual needs and culture. Most of the steps fall into two groups.

1. Identification of some essential components of the evaluation (the odd-numbered items)
2. Weighting and placing into priority order those essential components (the even-numbered items)

For convenience, we'll examine the Arreola model as a sequence of four pairs of steps: faculty roles, observable behaviors, appropriate sources, and system implementation.

Faculty Roles

While most academics immediately think of faculty responsibilities as divided among the three categories of teaching, scholarship, and service, even that familiar structure has a great deal of variability. What the term *scholarship* means at a large research university will be something quite different from what it means at a small liberal arts college. Moreover, even within those two institutions, the concept of research will vary greatly from discipline to discipline. The type of scholarship that a biologist does is not at all the same as what a sculptor does, and both of those are different from the scholarship of a historian. For this reason, faculty roles are best defined at the disciplinary level of each college or university in order to reflect the precise duties expected of any given faculty member.

In order to capture what faculty members really do (as opposed to relying on formal job descriptions, which tend to be overly general and not particularly helpful), Arreola (2007) recommends having each person draw up an inventory of his or her own work-related activities:

> [The specific duties of each person in the discipline are] determined by taking an inventory of actual activities in which the faculty engage in pursuing their professional responsibilities. In this step faculty can generally easily identify the activities that, for them, define the traditional roles of teaching, scholarly and creative activities, service, and administration or management. Experience has shown that faculty may also identify other important roles that must be included in the design of the faculty evaluation system [p. 2].

Arreola then provides forms that individual instructors can use to identify their activities as faculty members. The first form directs instructors to list every work-related function they can think of, using a two- to four-word title to summarize that responsibility. A second form is then developed at the departmental level and groups common activities into major categories, such as the standard academic triad of teaching, scholarship, and service, as well as other large categories that may be appropriate to that particular discipline, such as outreach to industry, fundraising, and mentoring of alumni. This second form reflects the consensus of faculty members within the discipline as to what being a college professor means in that field and at that institution. If possible, the department should burrow down into each major role or activity at least one or two layers in order to define more precisely the nature of each role or activity. For example, Arreola provides a hypothetical example of a discipline that defines the major roles of faculty members as teaching, scholarly and creative activities, professional recognition, and service. Moving down one level, teaching is defined as including instructional design, instructional delivery, and instructional assessment. Then, moving down a second level, instructional design is defined as developing course materials, developing computer simulations or exercises, and designing strategies for experiential learning projects (Arreola, 2007, Fig. 1.1). When this level of specificity is reached, step 1 in the process is complete.

Step 2 consists of determining how important to the discipline each of those roles or activities is perceived to be. This step can be accomplished in a number of ways. The most familiar method of assigning weights to each category is to use fixed percentages, such as teaching 50 percent, scholarship 40 percent, and service 10 percent. But certain disciplines may find this level of specificity too confining, and so a more dynamic weighting system may be more appropriate. In this type of system, each role or activity is assigned a range of weights, and values within those ranges are selected so that they add up to 100 percent. Arreola provides the example of a college with a strong teaching mission that assigns the ranges as follows: teaching, 50 to 85 percent; scholarly and creative activities, 0 to 35 percent; service to the college, 10 to 25 percent; and service to the general community, 5 to 10 percent.

Arreola is quick to point out that no matter which weighting system is used, the percentages should reflect the importance of that activity, not the assignment of load. For instance, in the hypothetical example we've just considered, "an individual faculty member may or may not have a full-time teaching load, but the value associated with teaching performance in this evaluation system could range from 50% to 85%" (Arreola, 2007, p. 10). Arreola recommends that the specific percentages within a dynamic weighting system be set at the departmental level and that the institution use these ranges as source material for a composite range that applies to the entire institution. That composite range should, in general terms, reflect institutional mission. In other words, a school that fits into the Carnegie Classification for a Research University with Very High Research Activity, but with higher composite ranges for teaching than for scholarship, may wish to reconsider whether its interpretation of faculty roles truly reflects the primary focus of the institution.

Observable Behaviors

After having drilled down two levels beneath such faculty roles as teaching, scholarship, and service, it may appear that we've already accomplished step 3 (define the roles in the faculty role model). After all, such activities as developing course materials or designing strategies for experiential learning projects seem to be specific, observable behaviors that we would now be in a position to evaluate. But as Arreola (2007) notes, what constitutes effective course materials in one discipline or at one level of depth in the discipline may well be quite different from another:

> Teaching a basic psychology course in a large lecture hall is different from teaching a lab course in biology is different from teaching a vocational course in air conditioner manufacturing on the floor of a factory. Teaching a graduate course is different from teaching an undergraduate course. Some faculty define meeting and counselling students as part of teaching. Librarians consider the orientation seminars they give to students and new faculty as teaching. Thus, to say we are going to evaluate teaching doesn't necessarily mean the same thing to everyone—even though we may all agree that it is important to evaluate it [p. 17].

Moreover, it's not yet clear what evidence we should examine in order to decide whether a faculty member's teaching meets our expectations for quality. As I noted in Chapters Three and Six, student course evaluations don't reveal very much about someone's level of expertise in content knowledge. Nor can peer evaluations reveal very much about patterns of teaching that emerged over the entire term since they're usually based on observing only one or two classes. For this reason, Arreola suggests refining the roles and activities even further until we can identify observable and measurable behaviors that form the basis of our evaluations. For example, one indicator of effectiveness in creating course materials might be "develops and uses learning objectives in designing effective learning experiences" (Arreola, 2007, p. 25). We now have something specific that we can observe: Does the faculty member include statements of expected learning outcomes on the course syllabus or not? Do these outcomes inform the quizzes, exams, and other documents associated with the course or not? In a similar way, Arreola outlines behaviors associated with what he calls the "performance skills" of teaching:

- Speaks clearly
- Is organized when making a presentation
- Uses personal examples when teaching
- Uses humor effectively
- Creates an appropriate psychological environment for learning [2007, p. 25]

Scholarship and service are similarly broken down into specific, observable behaviors, such as "making keynote or invited addresses" or "serving as a conference organizer" (Arreola, 2007, pp. 27, 28). Once again, these items aren't presented to serve as examples of best practices to be imitated, but merely as illustrations from which disciplines and institutions can develop their own sets of observable behavior, based on the pedagogy, research methods, mission, and function that are appropriate for their faculty's specific situation. In this way, the problem that we encountered before is now solved: what constitutes an observable behavior of excellence in scholarship at a comprehensive state university will be significantly different from the activities appropriate to a seminary or conservatory. Arreola also builds on Boyer's four types of scholarship (see Chapter Nine) by suggesting others that may suit the type of research faculty members in certain academic environments perform—for example:

- The scholarship of proficiency, which involves keeping up to date with the research of others and the latest modes of thought in one's field
- The scholarship of dissemination, which involves publication, presentation, and the explanation of research findings to experts and nonexperts alike
- The scholarship of translation, which involves "translating research findings into new products, services, or artistic expressions of benefit to either the professional or the larger general society" (Arreola, 2007, p. 27)

By carefully defining the specific activities that faculty members engage in when they demonstrate excellence in teaching, scholarship, and service, Arreola notes that evaluation, which has the potential for being a highly subjective process, can become demonstrably more objective. For example, people could argue endlessly about whether a certain professor has performed enough service, but it is easily recognizable whether someone has served as a journal editor or been an officer in a professional organization.

Once a suitable list of observable behaviors has been established, it's time once again to place individual items in priority order and assign them weights. Here too it's possible to adopt either fixed or variable percentages. In a fixed weighting system, each cluster of observable behaviors (Arreola calls them "role components") would be assigned specific values based on the priorities of the system. Arreola cites the example of a hypothetical institution where teaching is evaluated by giving the behaviors associated with instructional design a weight of 40 percent, those associated with instructional delivery a weight of 30 percent, those associated with instructional assessment a weight of 25 percent, and those associated with course management a weight of 5 percent. In a variable weighting system, individual disciplines would be permitted to adjust the weights of different activities in a manner that suited their specific priorities as long as together they total 100 percent. So an institution might assign the behaviors involved in the scholarship of proficiency anywhere from 50 to 100 percent, while those involved in the scholarship of discovery or creativity, the scholarship of dissemination, and the scholarship of translation each have a value somewhere between 0 and 50 percent. In this way, the discipline is able to take account of its own priorities while still reflecting the overall priorities of the institution as a whole.

Appropriate Sources

Steps 5 and 6 reflect a principle that we've often seen before: not every source of information about a faculty member's performance is equally reliable about everything we need to know. Arreola suggests that review committees prepare a grid on which the role components established in step 5 be listed in the left-most column, while the possible sources of information are listed across the topmost row. If we use the example of a variable weighting system for forms of scholarship, the initial blank grid would look something like Table 10.1.

We would then go through each cell on the grid and ask: Is the source that heads this column a good and valid source of information about the role component that heads this row? For example, is a self-evaluation a good and valid source of information about the faculty member's scholarship of proficiency? Are students a good and valid source of information about a faculty member's scholarship of proficiency? When the process is complete, all of the cells in the example contain the word *yes* or *no*. In the example, a review committee might

Table 10.1 Sources of Information About Scholarship

	Self	Students	Peers	Supervisor	Alumni	Parents	External Reviewers
Scholarship of proficiency							
Scholarship of discovery or creativity							
Scholarship of dissemination							
Scholarship of translation							

decide that students, alumni, and parents aren't valid sources of information about the quality of any type of scholarship, while peers and the faculty member's supervisor (usually his or her department chair) are useful sources of information about the quality of all types of scholarship, external reviewers most helpful in evaluating the quality of the scholarship of discovery or creativity and of dissemination, though not as helpful in evaluating the other two types. Similarly, the committee may decide that self-evaluations are useful for comparison purposes and to put information into its proper context, but not really helpful as sources of objective and unbiased information. This process is repeated for teaching, service, or any other role components that were identified as significant in the previous step.

Once these reliable sources have been identified, the committee then needs to determine the weight that will be placed on each source. So if a committee decides, for example, that students, peers, and the faculty member's chair are the three valid sources of information about the quality of a person's instructional delivery, the next logical question is: Do all three of these sources receive equal emphasis? The committee may believe that for this part of the evaluation, the students' perspective is the most important since they witness every class, whereas peers and the chair may sit in on only one or two. In other words, it may be appropriate in this situation to assign student observations 50 percent of the weight, peers 40 percent, and the chair 10 percent. At this point the committee has two sets of weights:

- The weight that each role component has in evaluating each specific role of a faculty member, such as teaching being evaluated on the basis of instructional design (40 percent), instructional delivery (50 percent), and instructional assessment (10 percent).
- The weight that each source of information has on each role component, such as instructional delivery being appraised by students (50 percent), peers (40 percent), and the chair (10 percent).

By taking the source percentage of the role component percentage, you get a combined value indicating how much emphasis should be placed on each source's rating of each group of behaviors in the overall evaluation of that faculty responsibility. Arreola terms this value the *composite role rating*. Performing this calculation sounds far more complicated than it is. For instance, in the hypothetical example we have considered, we saw that students would be relied on for 50 percent of the evaluation of the faculty member's instructional delivery, which itself was 50 percent of how we'd evaluate that person's teaching. Fifty percent of 50 percent is 25 percent. Thus, when we calculate a faculty member's overall evaluation in teaching, the students' rating of that instructor's instructional design should make up 25 percent of our total score. The chair provided only 10 percent of the evaluation of the faculty member's instructional delivery, which again was 50 percent of how we'd evaluate that person's teaching: 10 percent of 50 percent is 5 percent. So when we calculate a faculty member's overall evaluation in teaching, the chair's rating of that instructor's instructional design should make up only 5 percent of the total score.

Once you perform this type of calculation a few times, determining the overall weight of each component becomes quite easy. (It's even easier if you design a spreadsheet to make all of the calculations for you.) In addition, Arreola provides examples of Web sites in use at Fairmont State University where the calculations are performed automatically once the raw information has been entered.

System Implementation

Step 7 consists of identifying and using the mechanisms for obtaining information from each reliable source. In other words, if we say that students are a valid source of information about the quality of a faculty member's instructional delivery, how will we determine what students think? How will we determine what peers think? And how will we convert those impressions into a form that we can use as a component of the faculty member's overall rating? Arreola (2007) suggests several means to gather information from students—for example:

- Interview each student.
- Interview a random sample of students from each class.
- Administer a questionnaire or rating form to a random sample of students from each class.
- Administer a rating form to each student.

But each of these approaches has certain disadvantages. At a large university, interviewing every student would be impossible, while in a studio music program where lessons are provided one-on-one, there is no random sample of each class that we could obtain. We could certainly administer a rating form to each student (and most institutions have adopted this option), but unless we specifically ask about a particular issue, we're unlikely to learn much about it; besides, the halo effect (see Chapter Seven) tends to give well-liked or popular professors high scores across the board, regardless of how well they perform in the area covered by any specific question.

The best possible approach therefore is to combine a number of ways of obtaining information so that their various strengths will complement one another. In this way, rating forms administered to all students might be accompanied by interviews conducted with a small cross-section of the students. Arreola provides an extensive comparison of the strengths, weakness, and optimal conditions for effective use for such sources of information as student rating forms, tests of student performance, observations of simulated teaching, self-evaluations, department chair observations, peer ratings, and reviews by external specialists. In a similar way, it's possible to use multiple sources of reliable information to draw a fuller picture of a faculty member's success in research, service, and any other activity central to his or her responsibilities in the discipline. Braskamp and Ory (1994) provide insight into best practices for gathering reliable evidence from several common sources when conducting faculty reviews.

The Overall Composite Rating

Just as the weight given to each role component and the bearing that each source of information has on that component were used to determine an overall rating for each major role of a faculty member (the composite role rating), so does Arreola use two pieces of data to calculate what he terms the *overall composite rating*: a single figure that indicates each faculty member's success at performing his or her essential functions at the institution. The overall composite rating is calculated as the sum of all composite role ratings multiplied by the weight given that role in step 2. Let's consider a faculty member whose composite role ratings are 3.58 in an institution where 50 percent of the evaluation's weight is given to teaching; 2.36 in scholarship, which is given a weight of 40 percent; and 3.88 in service, which is given a weight of 10 percent. The overall composite rating for this faculty member would be calculated as shown in Table 10.2.

These overall composite ratings can be used synchronically (to compare one faculty member to another in a given year, as you might do in a summative evaluation) or diachronically (to measure a faculty member's progress or lack thereof, as you might in a formative evaluation).

Table 10.2 Overall Composite Rating

	Composite Role Rating	Weight	Calculation	Result
Teaching	3.58	50 percent	3.58 × .50	1.79
Scholarship	2.36	40 percent	2.36 × .40	.94
Service	3.88	10 percent	3.88 × .10	.39
Calculation				Sum of the above three values=
Overall composite rating				3.12

○ advantages and disadvantages of the arreola model

The model that Arreola proposed in *Developing a Comprehensive Faculty Evaluation System* has been field-tested at many colleges and universities, including Fairmont State University in West Virginia, Frostburg State University in Maryland, and St. Ambrose University in Iowa. Because it requires faculty members at both the department and institution levels to reflect on their precise roles and responsibilities, it's extremely useful in prompting the discussion of several key questions:

- What precisely is it that faculty members do in their individual disciplines and at this school?
- Which of those activities do we regard as most important?
- How do those activities relate to the mission of this institution?
- What sources of data are most reliable for us to determine the effectiveness of a faculty member's performance?

The Arreola model also has the potential for reducing the amount of subjectivity in what is necessarily a subjective process. It emphasizes the different components of an evaluation exactly as the institution itself defines their importance and produces numerical results that make it easy to compare the performance of faculty members even if their disciplines are quite different. It prompts discussions at each level of the institution about exactly what they are reviewing and why. And it holds great appeal for members of review committees, who feel more comfortable approaching a question by seeing it in quantitative terms.

Nevertheless, the Arreola model may not be for everyone. Faculty members in the humanities may well feel that its emphasis on quantifying information distorts the true complexity of the faculty experience. Indeed, with the values of the composite role rating and overall composite rating calculated to a hundredth of a point, it can be easy to overinterpret the data produced by the Arreola model. In other words, is a faculty member whose overall composite rating is 3.17 really "better" than someone who receives a 3.15? Moreover, since many rating forms require the reviewer to respond with whole numbers (1, 2, 3, 4, or 5 and not any fraction between 1 and 5), the caution against calculating means instead of medians that was discussed in Chapter Two needs to be kept in mind.

With the size of most data pools used in evaluations, the results are probably not statistically significant beyond one-tenth of a point or even a whole point. Figures as seemingly precise as the scores generated by the Arreola model may give the illusion of reliability without actually being all that reliable, particularly when reviewers are not statistically savvy. (See Chapter Two on this warning. In addition, remember that even the most carefully tested quantitative model can't eliminate all the subjectivity that is inherent in faculty evaluation.) Finally, this model is most effective when the entire institution adopts it, a challenge that can be difficult at large, complex institutions.

○ benefiting from the arreola model regardless of your current procedures

The Arreola model of faculty evaluation is most useful when an entire institution adopts it. Only then do you reap the full advantages from receiving a large body of comparison data. After all, if you evaluate a few faculty members in isolation, what does an overall composite rating of 2.87 mean? Is that better than we should expect, worse than we should expect, or roughly equivalent to what we should expect?

Nevertheless, there are ways to derive some of the benefits from the Arreola model even if no one else is using it at your college or university. For one thing, you can use this approach to develop a clearer sense of how strongly you should support one application relative to another. You can do this quickly by proceeding immediately to estimating your own composite role ratings and using them to calculate a rough overall composite rating. For instance, if you'd rate faculty member A as a 4 in teaching, a 3 in scholarship, and a 2 in service, with faculty member B receiving a 2 in teaching, a 3 in scholarship, and a 4 in service, your initial impulse might be to rate them as roughly equal since you gave them the same scores in each of the three main areas of evaluation even though these numbers were assigned to different categories. But if your institutional policy is that teaching carries 55 percent of the weight, scholarship 40 percent, and service 5 percent, your results will be very different. Faculty member A's composite score is 3.5 (55 percent of 4 is 2.2, 40 percent of 3 is 1.2, and 5 percent of 2 is .1; 2.2 + 1.2 + 0.1 = 3.5), while faculty member B rates only a 2.5 (55 percent of 2 is 1.1, 40 percent of 3 is 1.2, and 5 percent of 4 is .2; 1.1 + 1.2 + 0.2 = 2.5). In other words, the Arreola method can help you incorporate your own institution's priorities into your evaluations even if no one else is using it.

In a similar way, you could use the way in which Arreola calculates the core composite rating to be more consistent and objective in the way that you perform evaluations. The model causes you to think very carefully about the sources of information you use, how reliable they are, and how much emphasis you wish to give them. When you are examining someone's teaching, for instance, the method leads you to ask the following questions:

- What do we really mean at this institution and in this discipline by excellence in teaching? How do we recognize it when we see it?
- What are the sources of information we use to recognize those factors I've just identified?
- How important is each of those sources relative to one another?
- How reliable is each source likely to be?

By asking yourself these questions, you'll probe more deeply into the full nature of superior teaching instead of relying on the first source of data that you have at hand—usually student ratings of instruction— merely because it gives you a definite number, regardless of whether that number is reliable and indicative of everything you need to know. As Robert Diamond (2004) observes:

> Although more comprehensive assessment strategies are now emerg- ing, evaluation of teaching has depended heavily in the past on student ratings. Such measures, while useful, provide only one vision of teacher effectiveness. You should keep in mind that student evalu- ations are usually collected near the end of the term when many of the failing or unhappy students are no longer in attendance or when those who have remained in class are anxious about final grades [p. 24].

You can ask questions based on the Arreola model independent of other reviewers as you develop your own ratings, or you can use them to help guide a committee's deliberations as they review an entire set of applications.

mini-case studies: the arreola model

Based on the mission of your own institution, what weights would you assign each of the following faculty roles if you had to use the variable weighting system outlined below? If your institution has faculty members with clearly distinct roles (for example, teaching faculty whose assignments are significantly different from those of the research faculty), choose the role that tends to be most common in your own discipline. Remember that the sum of all your choices must add up to 100 percent.

1. Teaching: 20–60 percent
2. Research: 10–50 percent
3. Service to the academic discipline: 5–25 percent
4. Service to the community: 0–25 percent
5. Collegiality: 0–15 percent

o o o

Based on your own academic field, what weights would you assign each of the following components of scholarship if you had to use the variable weighting system outlined below? Once again, remember that the sum of all your choices must add up to 100 percent:

1. External grant activity: 0–50 percent
2. Publication of research articles in first-tier journals: 0–50 percent
3. Publication of research articles in other journals: 0–50 percent
4. Publication of scholarly books: 0–75 percent
5. Conference attendance: 0–10 percent
6. Conference presentations: 0–20 percent
7. Artistic production or performance: 0–80 percent
8. The scholarship of teaching and learning: 0–40 percent
9. Other forms of scholarship (please specify) 0–100 percent
10. Currency with developments in discipline: 10–75 percent

o o o

Implement the Arreola model in Table 10.2 by calculating the three core composite indicators (Table 10.3) and the overall composite rating (Table

(Continued)

10.4) for the hypothetical faculty member whose scores are provided. Unlike other mini-case studies in this book, this problem has only one correct solution. For the answers, see Tables 10.5 and 10.6 at the end of the chapter in the "Solutions to Mini-Case Study" section.

Table 10.3 Core Composite Indicators

Roles and Components	Weight	Score	Weight × Score
Teaching: 50%			
Instructional design	10%	3.8	
Instructional delivery	40%	3.4	
Instructional assessment	20%	1.1	
Mastery of content	25%	3.8	
Resource management	5%	2.7	
Total	100%		
Scholarship: 40%			
Publications	40%	3.7	
Grant activity	40%	2.0	
Conference presentations	15%	3.2	
Fostering undergraduate research	5%	2.9	
Total	100%		
Service: 10%			
Service to the department	50%	3.9	
Service to the institution	10%	3.4	
Service to the field	30%	2.3	
Service to the community	10%	.7	
Total	100%		

Table 10.4 Calculation of the Composite Role Rating

	Composite Role Rating	Weight	Result
Teaching		50%	
Scholarship		40%	
Service		10%	
Calculation			Sum of the above three values =
Overall composite rating			

○ conclusion

The Arreola model may be regarded as a means of quantifying the unquantifiable. It tends to appeal to reviewers who come from disciplines in which numerical analysis is common or who prefer specific, clear values to descriptive terms like "superb," "excellent," and "outstanding." It has great value in compelling disciplines and institutions to consider in depth how their missions affect what they regard as important among the various activities that define faculty responsibilities and which sources of information are most effective in providing those insights. While the model is particularly valuable when adopted institution-wide, it also has use in individual departments and even for individual reviewers.

References

Arreola, R. A. (2007). *Developing a comprehensive faculty evaluation system: A guide to designing, building, and operating large-scale faculty evaluation systems.* San Francisco: Jossey-Bass/Anker.

Braskamp, L. A., & Ory, J. C. (1994). *Assessing faculty work: Enhancing individual and institutional performance.* San Francisco: Jossey-Bass.

Diamond, R. M. (2004). *Preparing for promotion, tenure, and annual review: A faculty guide* (2nd ed.). San Francisco: Jossey-Bass/Anker.

Resources

Diamantes, T. (2002, October 9). *Review of Arreola, Raoul (2000). Developing a comprehensive faculty evaluation system: A handbook for college faculty and administrators on designing and operating a comprehensive faculty evaluation system*, 2nd ed., Bolton, MA: Anker. Retrieved from http://www.edrev.info/reviews/rev189.htm.

Paulsen, M. (2002). Evaluating teaching performance. *New Directions for Institutional Research, 114*, 5–18.

○ solution to mini-case study

Allow for some slight variation in your answers depending on how you rounded fractions to the nearest hundredth. Also, because calculations of this type are unlikely to be significant to the hundredths place, this faculty member should be rated an overall 3 on a four-point scale.

Table 10.5 Solutions: Scores for Roles and Components

Roles and Components	Weight	Score	Weight × Score
Teaching: 50%			
Instructional design	10%	3.8	.38
Instructional delivery	40%	3.4	1.36
Instructional assessment	20%	1.1	.22
Mastery of content	25%	3.8	.95
Resource management	5%	2.7	.14
Total	100%		3.05
Scholarship: 40%			
Publications	40%	3.7	1.48
Grant activity	40%	2.0	.8
Conference presentations	15%	3.2	.48

Table 10.6 Score for Overall Composite Rating

	Composite Role Rating	Weight	Result
Teaching	3.05	50%	1.52
Scholarship	2.9	40%	1.16
Service	3.05	10%	.3
Calculation			Sum of the above three values =
Overall composite rating			2.99

11

the seldin model

If the process that Raoul Arreola developed, which we explored in Chapter Ten, represents a fully developed model of the quantitative approach to faculty evaluation, the process that Peter Seldin developed might be regarded as its qualitative equivalent. Seldin serves as Distinguished Professor of Management Emeritus at Pace University in Pleasantville, New York. His perspective on faculty evaluation has been shaped by both his work as a professor of management and his former responsibilities as a department chair and academic dean. Seldin has promoted his ideas through a number of books, including *Changing Practices in Evaluating Teaching* (1999) and *Evaluating Faculty Performance* (2006), as well as his work on portfolio evaluation, such as *The Teaching Portfolio* (2010, with Elizabeth Miller and Clement Seldin), *Successful Use of Teaching Portfolios* (1993), and *The Academic Portfolio* (2009, with Elizabeth Miller). In 2002, Seldin expanded his evaluation model to administrators in *The Administrative Portfolio*, coauthored with Mary Lou Higgerson. The fundamental tool at the heart of the Seldin model is the portfolio: a reflective, evidence-based set of materials that documents a faculty member's achievements.

Seldin's portfolio concept is based on two central premises. First, the best sort of faculty evaluation is that which encourages those under review to reflect seriously on what they've done in their professional positions, why they've done it, how their progress has developed over their careers, and which improvements seem most desirable in the future. Second, quantitative analysis can't tell reviewers the whole story. Numbers frequently lack context, and it's often impossible to tell, for instance, whether someone's average score on student evaluations has declined from 3.7 to 3.5 to 3.1 to 2.9 over four years because he or she has become less effective as a teacher or because other factors are involved. It could be that a significant change in the faculty member's life has resulted in a temporary decline over these years, but that we can soon expect his or her scores to return to their earlier values. It may be that the faculty member's course assignment has changed during this period or that the students in his or her courses have changed from being majors who were enthusiastic about the material to being students from other fields who are reluctantly fulfilling a widely disliked general education requirement. It may be that the form on which students record their evaluations has changed or that other factors are at work that aren't immediately obvious to a reviewer. Because of so many potential variables, quantitative analysis alone can't provide insights into the full context of the results; portfolios can.

Barbara Millis (1991), formerly of the University of Maryland and now director of the Teaching and Learning Center at the University of Texas at San Antonio, cites five reasons that a portfolio approach to faculty evaluation is useful:

- Portfolios are cost-effective. "Individual departments unable to initiate more costly teaching reforms such as extensive TA training or reduction of class sizes, can still initiate a portfolio process by rethinking and reallocating faculty time and commitment. . . . To develop a viable . . . portfolio program, the ultimate investments must be made, of course, by the individual faculty members assembling the . . . portfolios. . . . Concentrated effort spread out over parts of only a few days can result in a viable, self-tailored document which can then be further shaped over time as . . . improvements occur. . . . As a matter of practicality, . . . portfolios, if they are to be embraced by faculty, must be manageable and cost effective" (pp. 219–220).

- Since portfolios originate at the departmental level, they can reflect the distinctive aspects of that discipline. While it's likely that all the portfolios developed at an institution will adhere to a standard format, there's still some flexibility within those parameters that allows disciplines to focus on the activities most important to them. Moreover, since portfolios require a great deal of reflection on the part of the faculty member, they make it much easier for disciplines to explain aspects of their work that they don't share with other academic fields so that outsiders can understand these distinctive elements more easily.

- Portfolios counter the superficiality of other types of evaluation that focus exclusively on results and don't provide insight into context, patterns over time, and causal factors. For example, "the teaching portfolio, with its rich content emphasizing the products of good teaching, with its reflective commentary and course materials, and with its information and observations from others, can provide solid evidence about the quality of teaching effectiveness" (Millis, 1991, p. 221). If quantitative methods of evaluation are extremely useful in indicating what a faculty member's level of performance was, portfolios are more effective in showing why that result occurred. From portfolios, review committees can determine which features of someone's course materials made these items successful (or unsuccessful) learning tools, which features of someone's scholarship were (or were not) innovative, and which features of someone's service had (or didn't have) a significant impact on others.

- Portfolios engage faculty members directly in the process of documentation and reflection. Unlike other systems of evaluation for which a great deal of information—such as teaching assignments, summaries of course evaluations, external letters of review, and the like—can be collected by the committee with little or no participation by those who are being reviewed, portfolios require the faculty

member's active involvement at every stage. Moreover, that involvement consists or more than merely gathering information to meet
a requirement. It requires the faculty member to give careful consideration to the way in which he or she documents achievements,
thus making the portfolio process a valuable activity of introspec-
tion and learning.

• Portfolios promote consultation and collaboration. By their very
nature, portfolios are quite difficult for anyone to prepare on his or
her own. They almost always require the faculty member to involve
others in the process of selecting and evaluating materials, thus
encouraging a broader discussion about what constitutes success in
each of the areas under evaluation.

○ the nature of a portfolio

In many evaluation systems, faculty members and committees believe
that they're already using portfolios. As an administrator, you can
provide leadership by correcting this false impression. A large amount
of materials is collected at most universities, placed in binders, and then
examined by the person's supervisor or review committee. But these
binders aren't the sort of portfolio Seldin has in mind. In the attempt
to document everything, the multiple binders that are in common use
end up documenting nothing particularly well. No one has time to read
hundreds and hundreds of pages of material gathered in this way, and
so important documents become overlooked in the welter of material.
Moreover, binders have the appearance of giving every item the same
importance as every other item they contain, leading people to joke that
evaluation materials "aren't read anymore; they're simply weighed"
(Buller, 2007). In contrast to this process of simply collecting raw information, a genuine portfolio has three distinct features.

First, it is selective. Instead of encouraging faculty members to
dump every bit of documentation on a review committee, portfolios
require faculty members to choose materials that are particularly revealing or significant. For instance, a good portfolio wouldn't contain every
syllabus that a faculty member has developed but perhaps the three best

syllabi he or she ever prepared. Rather than including copies of every article the candidate wrote, the portfolio might contain the faculty member's five most important articles. Instead of merely listing all the committees on which he or she served, the faculty member might be asked to describe the service work that made the most difference. In this way, the reviewer gains insight into what the faculty member regards as important and is spared the need to try to determine his or her priorities from a large amount of documentation that has little form or structure. As Seldin et al. (2010) write:

> The teaching portfolio is not an exhaustive compilation of all the documents and materials that bear on teaching performance. Instead it culls from the record selected information on teaching activities and solid evidence of their effectiveness. Just as in a curriculum vitae, all claims in the portfolio should be supported by firm empirical evidence. Selectivity is important because the portfolio should not be considered a huge repository of indiscriminate documentation. Rather, it should be seen as a judicious, critical, purposeful analysis of performance, evidence, and goals [pp. 4–5].

Second, a portfolio is reflective. It contains statements from the faculty member about why he or she considers the chosen syllabi especially good, the articles important, and the service contributions meaningful. This type of reflection can take a number of forms. One of the most common is a statement of philosophy that begins each major section of the review. Although statements about the philosophy of teaching, scholarship, and service are most important, it's also possible to structure the portfolio around other major criteria that are appropriate to that institution. In this way, a portfolio might contain a statement about the faculty member's philosophy of collegiality, innovation, or academic leadership. Religious colleges might require a faith statement, medical schools a statement about the person's philosophy of patient care, and so on. Moreover, statements of philosophy aren't the only ways in which portfolios can be reflective. It's also possible for the candidate to provide a syllabus for a course as it was taught five or ten years ago, followed by a syllabus from that same course today, with an explanation about why he or she implemented certain changes. Publications and course materials can be annotated to clarify what the faculty member was trying to accomplish in various sections of each document, whether he or she regards those attempts as successful, and how he or she might do things differently if that document were being developed today. In other words, there's no set form in which the reflective elements of the portfolio have to be conveyed as long as they're appropriate to the discipline and institution.

Finally, a portfolio is formative and summative. The very process of reflection that goes into developing a portfolio makes it formative. The faculty member must consider at each stage how he or she has improved in the past and how this pattern of progress will be continued in the future. But portfolios are also extremely valuable in summative processes. If a faculty member says that a particular set of materials represents his or her best work, it becomes quite easy for the discipline and institution to decide whether these efforts were truly good enough to warrant a positive decision. In other words, are these products of scholarship really at the quality we expect associate professors to demonstrate? Are these exams, which the faculty member said were examples of his or her most creative classroom materials, at the level we'd want our tenured full professors to be producing? While certain quantitative processes might tell you that a given faculty member was achieving less impressive results in, for example, teaching than in research and service or is ranking lower overall than other members of the institution, a portfolio can give a reviewer an understanding of why these results occurred, whether a sufficient amount of improvement is likely to be possible within a reasonable amount of time, and what sort of remediation the person may require.

○ the contents of a portfolio

The portfolios used in faculty review and evaluation generally fall into one of two categories: teaching portfolios (which deal with documentation related to instruction only) and academic portfolios (which address every major faculty responsibility relevant to the review). Taken as a whole, the portfolio should tell a consistent story—what I call *the narrative*—that allows the reviewer to understand the faculty member's achievements and why they're important—that matter of worth that we explored in Chapter Seven.

Aside from this consistent narrative, however, there are very few requirements about what the portfolio must contain. Evaluators must avoid the tendency to evaluate the content of one portfolio in terms of another. You may first be reading a set of documents that contains a superbly written statement of how and why the faculty member made certain curricular revisions, while the next sets you examine lack such a statement. Unless your policies specifically state that portfolios must contain certain items, allowing one portfolio to set the standard for content when examining others is a poor practice.

Every faculty member has a career trajectory that is different from everyone else. The primary focus needs to be whether the contents adequately document the narrative and whether that narrative relates to the faculty member's role at the institution and the criteria of the decision being made. What is the person under review trying to tell you in order to persuade you to respond positively in your evaluation:

- Does the faculty member tend to view his or her strengths primarily in the area of teaching or research?
- How does he or she relate one of these areas to the other?
- What relationship does the person's service have to the other major contributions he or she has made?
- What sense do you gain from the materials about the faculty member's values, priorities, and goals for the future?

The first red flag you may encounter during a portfolio review is that this overall narrative is missing, inconsistent, not well related to the documentation provided, or irrelevant to the faculty member's primary duties or the institution's mission. In that case, the faculty member either did a poor job preparing the portfolio or hasn't been successful in contributing to the institution in an effective manner. Both of these possibilities are real problems, but how you handle them may be different. If the portfolio is poorly prepared, institutional policies may allow you to suggest certain revisions. If the faculty member's contributions have been weak, it's highly unlikely that the entire review will have a positive outcome.

○ what else to look for when reviewing a portfolio

Some reviewers find it extremely difficult to identify the quality of a faculty member's work if they are not examining a numerical score but rather a set of documents that may look very different from what another person has submitted. If you or someone else serving on the review committee is encountering this problem, the solution may be to focus attention first on the overall narrative and then on the portfolio's success in documentation. Has the faculty member supported his or her achievements with adequate evidence? For example, if the person under review presents a narrative claiming that he or she is a dynamic, innovative teacher but then supplies as samples of classroom materials only multiple-choice exams that came prepackaged with the textbook, there's a significant inconsistency between the claims that were made and the documentation that was provided. Similarly, if the faculty member's goals describe intentions to apply for large grants and produce cutting-edge scholarship, but there's no documentation in the portfolio of activities that would lay the foundation for this kind of achievement, you should regard that discrepancy as a warning sign that should be investigated further.

Then try to determine historical patterns that emerge from the portfolio. Is the faculty member improving as an instructor, building an expanding program of research, and assuming the type of leadership positions that are appropriate for increasing seniority? If there are gaps in the record, plateaus in achievement, or deterioration of accomplishment in any area, are there mitigating factors (such as family challenges, a need to refocus his or her research priorities, or personal illness) that may explain these occurrences? Is the level of progress and achievement what your institution would normally expect for someone in that discipline with equivalent years of experience? In short, would you regard the person's career to be on an overall upward trajectory? If not, are there acceptable reasons for the pattern that you're seeing?

Finally, consider whether the faculty member has developed a reasonable plan for moving forward. Plans are, of course, always in flux. No one can predict accurately every development that'll occur in his or her discipline, every award and opportunity that'll come along, and every discovery that he or she is likely to make. But the faculty member's plan should be a well-considered road map based on current information and understanding. Remember that now is the time for a reviewer to examine these plans and conclude whether what the faculty member intends to do is enough to meet the expectations of the institution. Tacit acceptance of a flawed plan will simply give the faculty member approval for moving in a direction or at a pace that's unlikely to correspond to the needs of the discipline and institution. Even in a review process that's simply looking at past accomplishments (such as consideration of a faculty member for a campus award), there's a useful opportunity to provide the sort of mentoring that can help the person become even more successful in the future.

○ benefiting from the seldin model regardless of your current procedures

Even if your college or university doesn't require that portfolios be prepared for evaluations, there are still ways in which you as the reviewer can take advantage of Seldin's model. For example, a key strength of portfolios is that they encourage the faculty member to reflect on his or her achievements, not merely document them. As we've seen, this reflection can provide a better context for the information when you review it and make it clear why the faculty member has done something instead of just knowing what he or she has done. It may be possible to add some of this reflective practice to any type of faculty review. If there's an interview component of the evaluation before conclusions are drawn, questions can be directed to the applicant in such a way that they prompt the type of reflection one commonly sees in a portfolio:

- If you were teaching the same course as several of your colleagues, what would students receive from your approach that they may not receive from anyone else?
- Who were the biggest influences on how you teach? What did you learn from them?
- How has your teaching changed since your last review? Why did it change?
- What sources of information do you use to determine whether one of your teaching techniques is working?
- What do you regard as your most significant scholarly achievement? Why is that product particularly important?
- What about a particular scholarly or creative topic captures your interest enough to pursue it further?
- How is the world a better place because of the research you've performed?
- What was the most important thing you learned from a research project or activity that failed?
- How do you go about determining which committees you'll volunteer for or allow yourself to be placed on?
- Why do you think it's important for faculty members to engage in service?

Furthermore, it may be possible to incorporate into an existing review process the way in which the Seldin model uses reflection to inform goal setting. Gary Rolfe, a professor of nursing at Swansea University in England, suggests that the reflective process can be divided into three stages, each represented by a simple question (Rolfe, Freshwater, and Jasper, 2001):

1. *What?* ("Describe the precise nature of the activity that occurred.") In a faculty review, this question tends to be answered by the documentation itself that lists courses taught, student successes achieved, publications, grants received, committees on which the faculty member served, and so on.

2. *So what?* ("Why was what occurred important?") In a faculty review, this question can be addressed by having the faculty member discuss the significance of each activity and justify its priority. Although that information will be contained in a well-designed portfolio, in other situations you may need to ask this question directly of the individual and others reviewing that person.

3. *Now what?* ("Based on the achievements and their significance, what's the plan for the future?") In a portfolio, this type of goal setting emerges naturally from the faculty member's process of selection and reflection. In other situations, reviewers will often want to conclude even a purely summative process by making it formative in some way.

---

mini-case studies: the seldin model

Suppose that you're reviewing a teaching portfolio that contains the following statement of pedagogical philosophy: "True learning occurs only when students are actively engaged in the educational process. While it is important for students to master the basic facts and concepts of the discipline, the best education occurs when students are regularly challenged to think critically, consider issues from multiple perspectives, and challenge data for accuracy. When students complete my courses, I want them not merely to be closer to their degrees but also better equipped to obtain, assess, and apply information." When you review the faculty member's documentation, however, you notice that the only pedagogical technique the instructor explicitly describes as a classroom method is the lecture, all quizzes and exams are in multiple-choice and true/false formats, and all classroom materials are in text alone, with the information crammed tightly together on each page.

(Continued)

What would you do next to begin discovering what accounts for the apparent disconnect between the faculty member's statement and the documentation that was selected?

o   o   o

You're reviewing a portfolio in which the faculty member has included current syllabi paired with syllabi from the same course as it was taught ten years ago. To your surprise, you feel that the older syllabi are far better than the newer examples. The materials from a decade ago include many more requirements for out-of-class student writing and the class projects were far more imaginative. In the formal interview that the institution requires as part of the review, you ask the faculty member about this change. The response is: "Well, you know the budget cuts we've been through. I could teach the course like that when sections were capped at twenty or twenty-five students. But now a course considered small has fifty or seventy-five students in it. Plus with the increasing demands we're under to do research, I just can't devote that much time to the course outside the classroom. So I've cut way back on the amount of material we cover and designed quizzes and exams that my TA can grade. I had no other option."

Do you regard the professor's statement as sufficient justification for the change? Did other options exist? If this were a summative evaluation, is this response likely to have a negative impact on your decision? If it's a formative evaluation, what advice might you give?

o   o   o

A tenure-track faculty member who's undergoing a probationary pretenure review after three years of full-time service has submitted an academic portfolio to you. In the research section, you see a lot of information documenting attempts at producing a successful product of scholarship—article submissions, grant proposals, and book outlines—but no actual products. The articles were turned down, the grant proposals were rejected, and publishers have declined all the book outlines. You contact the faculty member for an informal mentoring session and ask about what you found in the portfolio. The response is: "I'm not going to publish just anywhere. You'll notice that all of my article submissions were in the most selective first-tier journals, and all the book outlines were sent to very prestigious university presses. The grants, too, were all multimillion-dollar proposals sent to important government agencies. I don't want to be just an ordinary faculty member; I'm trying to be the best in my field."

What long-term career advice might you pass along to the faculty member? What short-term suggestions might you make about revising the portfolio so as to increase the likelihood of a positive third-year review?

○ conclusion

The advantages of the Seldin model are that it can provide reviewers with a much better perspective into why faculty members made many of the decisions they did, offer those who assemble the portfolios an understanding of how they should improve in the future, and explain to reviewers from outside the discipline how the distinctive teaching and research methodologies of that field relate to the material being studied. The disadvantage is that subjectivity may be a very strong factor in the reviewer's judgment. Since portfolio evaluation doesn't result in a score, it can be difficult to determine the relative merits of different portfolios, particularly when the faculty members are from very diverse fields or have presented their materials (as they should) in very different ways. For this reason, some reviewers may feel that portfolio analysis is more effective in formative than summative evaluations or that they can enhance but not replace other methods of evaluation.

References

Buller, J. L. (2007). Improving documentation for promotion and tenure. *Academic Leader*, 23(11), 8–9.

Millis, B. J. (1991). Putting the teaching portfolio in context. In K.J.E. Zahorski (Ed.), *To improve the academy: Resources for student, faculty, and institutional development* (pp. 215–229). Stillwater, OK: New Forum Press.

Rolfe, G., Freshwater, D., & Jasper, M. (2001). *Critical reflection for nursing and the helping professions: A user's guide.* Houndmills, Basingstoke, Hampshire: Palgrave.

Seldin, P. (1993). *Successful use of teaching portfolios.* San Francisco: Jossey-Bass/Anker.

Seldin, P. (1999). *Changing practices in evaluating teaching: A practical guide to improved faculty performance and promotion/tenure decisions*. San Francisco: Jossey-Bass/ Anker.

Seldin, P. (2006). *Evaluating faculty performance: A practical guide to assessing teaching, research, and service*. San Francisco: Jossey-Bass/Anker.

Seldin, P., & Higgerson, M. L. (2002). *The administrative portfolio: A practical guide to improved administrative performance and personnel decisions*. San Francisco: Jossey-Bass/Anker.

Seldin, P., & Miller, J. E. (2009). *The academic portfolio: A practical guide to documenting teaching, research, and service*. San Francisco: Jossey-Bass.

Seldin, P., Miller, J. E., & Seldin, C. A. (2010). *The teaching portfolio: A practical guide to improved performance and promotion/tenure decisions* (4th ed.) San Francisco: Jossey-Bass.

12

incorporating quantitative and qualitative approaches into an integrated process

In Chapters Ten and Eleven, we saw that the Arreola model has the advantage of reducing (though never quite eliminating) the amount of subjectivity that can affect faculty reviews and evaluations, and the Seldin model has the advantage of providing a clearer context for a faculty member's most significant achievements and challenges. In this final chapter, we explore two useful ways in which you can combine the benefits derived from both these systems, regardless of whether your institution has adopted either of them for all faculty reviews. I'll also draw some conclusions based on everything discussed throughout the book and suggest how those conclusions can make you more effective and confident and less prone to grievances and legal challenges as a reviewer.

○ two possibilities for blending quantitative and qualitative approaches

The first way in which to incorporate aspects of both qualitative and quantitative analysis in an evaluation process is to borrow from the Seldin model the way in which faculty members collect, organize, and reflect on the supporting materials for a review, and then to borrow from the Arreola model the way in which consistent decisions are made based on this material.

In this first approach, the two models shape and inform one another. For example, you might begin a review by informing the faculty member about the various roles and weights that'll be used to perform the evaluation (steps 1 and 2 of the Arreola model). In this way, if a faculty member knows that teaching will count for 50 percent of the evaluation, scholarship 40 percent, and service 10 percent, he or she has valuable information about which materials to select for the portfolio. The teaching section should receive much more emphasis than the service section, with the scholarship section documented almost as thoroughly as the teaching section. Moreover, by informing the faculty member of the weights assigned to the various clusters of behavior within each major role (steps 3 and 4), as well as the weights assigned to different sources of information (steps 5 and 6), the person under review will have clear guidance about how his or her time should be spent while preparing the portfolio.

Suppose that letters of support from colleagues on a committee account for only 10 percent of the weight in evaluating the role component of committee activities, and committee activities account for only 20 percent of the faculty role of service, which in turn accounts for only 10 percent of the entire evaluation. This information would lead the faculty member to conclude that spending too much time soliciting letters from colleagues is not in his or her best interest. It would make a lot more sense to focus on annotating how he or she improved course syllabi over the years, since (in our hypothetical system) annotated course syllabi account for 60 percent of the weight in the role component of instructional design, and instructional design accounts for 40 percent of the faculty role of teaching, which in turn accounts for half of the entire evaluation.

Armed with this information, the faculty member can then use the Seldin model to create an academic portfolio that accurately addresses the issues that will be of greatest concern for the review committee. All of the advantages of reflection, selection, collaboration, and formative advice that are derived from the preparation of the portfolio then occur as the faculty member carefully chooses material that provides evidence of success in each key area and considers what can be learned from reviewing his or her own material. The preparation of the portfolio thus replaces Arreola's step 7. When the portfolio is completed and submitted for formal review, the committee then returns to the Arreola model to score the portfolio and develop an overall composite rating that can be used in comparing one candidate's portfolio to another (step 8).

That overall composite rating is valuable for making the actual decision in the evaluation process (the summative element), while individual role component ratings and core component ratings can guide the faculty development process (the formative element). Combined with the faculty member's own insights gained from the reflective dimension of the academic portfolio, this formative element becomes the basis for setting meaningful goals and planning growth for the future. In this way, our first integrated process can be illustrated as depicted in Figure 12.1.

The second way in which to combine both quantitative and qualitative methods into a single process is to play to the strengths of both methods. As we've seen, the strengths of the Arreola model are that it reduces subjectivity and provides a result that reflects the priorities of the discipline and institution. The strengths of the Seldin model are that it provides a better sense of context for achievements and explains why things occurred, not just what occurred. You can take advantage of these complementary strengths by using the Arreola model to quantify the quantifiable and the Seldin model to explain the explicable.

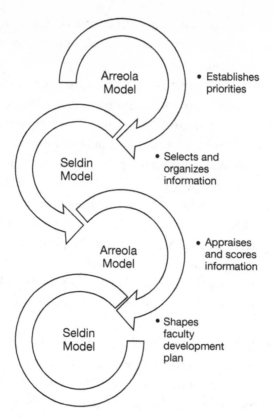

Figure 12.1 Integrated Model #1

Certain sources of information that are gathered for evaluations are easily reducible to numbers: scores on student or peer evaluations, number of referreed articles, size of external grants received, number of committee assignments, number of leadership positions held in professional organizations, and so on. These are the factors that are most easily examined in terms of a quantified result. Some of these factors don't even need to be converted in order to include them in a calculation based on the Arreola model. In most systems, for instance, student course evaluations and peer reviews are already scored on a system ranging from 0 to 4. (Keep in mind, once again, the reasons for using medians rather than means in most cases, as discussed in Chapter

Two.) Other factors can be converted into a similar score based on the priorities and mission of the institution. Depending on a school's research mission, for example, it might set up a formula similar to the following when addressing the external grants a faculty member has received:

a.	Over $5 million	4.0
b.	$3 million–$4.99 million	3.75
c.	$2 million–$2.99 million	3.5
d.	$1 million–$1.99 million	3.25
e.	$750,000–$999,999	3.0
f.	$500,000–$749,999	2.75
g.	$250,000–$499,999	2.5
h.	$100,000–$249,000	2.25
i.	$1–$99,999	2.0
j.	No grants received but proposals sent	1.0
k.	No grants received; no proposals sent	0.0

Other elements of the evaluation can be converted using similar formulas. The important thing, however, will be to develop these formulas before examining any individual's materials and in consultation with the disciplines involved. Once you begin examining actual cases, it's very difficult to eliminate bias favoring or disadvantaging specific individuals as the formulas are being developed. Then, when every easily quantifiable component of the documentation is converted into a number from 0 through 4, the numbers can be weighted and calculated to produce an overall composite rating as usual for the Arreola model.

Other aspects of the evaluation are much more difficult to quantify. How, for instance, do you quantify the improvement of a new syllabus over an old one? Certainly a rating rubric could be developed (and often must be developed for certain factors in the Arreola model), but then a greater degree of subjectivity, the very factor we were trying to reduce, can begin to creep in. For concepts as flexible as improvement, excellence, and the like, it can be extremely difficult to establish interrater reliability (the degree to which different observers produce the same results). It's far more productive to leave quantifiable elements of the evaluation for factors that can be measured and adopt the techniques of qualitative analysis for other factors.

It's in this regard that Seldin's portfolio model demonstrates its strengths. In fact, by moving back and forth between Seldin's and Arreola's models, it's possible to achieve a highly desirable balance between objectivity and clarity of context. In this way, if the composite role rating for a faculty member's teaching gradually increased over the past five years, you can look at the annotated syllabi and course materials, letters from students, and other materials in the candidate's academic portfolio to determine why that may have been the case.

Conversely, if in your review of the portfolio you sense that the individual's research productivity peaked at about the time he or she was promoted to the rank of associate professor and then plateaued or has declined ever since, you can examine the pattern of the faculty member's composite role ratings and role component ratings to verify whether that was indeed the case. (On the concepts of the composite role rating and role component rating, see Chapter Ten.) In this way, our second model for integrating quantitative and qualitative analysis might be illustrated as depicted in Figure 12.2.

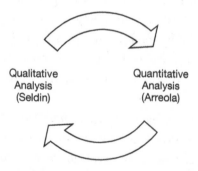

Qualitative   Quantitative
Analysis   Analysis
(Seldin)   (Arreola)

Figure 12.2 Integrated Model #2

o why an integrated approach is particularly useful at institutions with specialized faculty tracks

Some colleges and universities allow faculty members to select specialized tracks that affect both their evaluation criteria and workload. The most common system of specialized tracks offers three options:

1. *Balanced track.* Roughly equivalent emphasis is placed on both teaching and research.
2. *Research track.* Greater emphasis is placed on research than teaching.
3. *Teaching track.* Greater emphasis is placed on teaching than research.

As an example, here's how the specialized system is designed in the Neeley School of Business at Texas Christian University:

There are three general career tracks.

- *Balanced Track.* With this track teaching would generally include a 40–45% effort, research a 40–45% effort, and professional service a 10–20% effort.
- *Research Track.* This track would allow teaching effort to be 20–40%, research 50–70%, and professional service 10–25%.
- *Teaching Track.* With this track teaching is 60–80% of effort, research 10–15% of effort, and service 10–25% of effort.

Untenured regular faculty should be on a balanced track or research track for each year of their probationary period. Over their probationary period (untenured) they should place an equal or nearly equal emphasis on teaching and research. Determination of the specific track each year is related to departmental and school needs as well as the needs of the faculty member in making adequate progress toward tenure. A regular three-credit-hour course should count at least 10 percent and not more than 15 percent of annual effort [http://www.provost.tcu.edu/Tenure_and_Promotion/neeleycriteria.pdf].

The idea is that most three-credit courses count for 10 percent of a faculty member's workload assignment and weight in evaluations, with the possibility of increasing this amount to 15 percent when justified due to "very large class sizes, a graduate offering, very heavy writing or other requirements that require substantially higher effort on behalf of the faculty member. . . . In general a faculty member with a teaching emphasis will teach from 6 to 8 courses per academic year; a faculty member with a balanced emphasis will teach 4 to 5 courses per academic year; a faculty member with a research emphasis will teach 2 to 4 courses per academic year" (http://www.provost.tcu.edu/Tenure_and_Promotion/neeleycriteria.pdf). Once they are tenured, faculty members may move from one track to another for the duration of an entire academic year, although the assumption is that such shifts will be relatively rare; for most people, pursuing a balanced, research, or teaching track is expected to be a long-term decision.

Systems that allow specialized faculty tracks reflect the reality that not all faculty members are alike, although these systems also have the potential to complicate the evaluation process tremendously. In other words, faculty members are being evaluated on scales that include so many different weights—particularly when variable weighting systems are combined with multiple faculty tracks, as is the case in the example we considered—that it can be extremely difficult to "compare apples to apples." It's in these situations that the value of integrated processes of faculty evaluation really emerges. Arreola's model contains just the sort of flexibility needed to adjust formulas so that they can accommodate variable weights, while the overall composite rating provides a score that can be meaningfully compared to those of other faculty members. Seldin's model, with its emphasis on context and explanation, can serve to clarify to reviewers the significance of each achievement, the faculty member's rate of progress, and his or her goals for the future. In this way, evaluation processes can have the best of both worlds: maximum flexibility to reflect differing faculty roles and a consistent outcome that allows meaningful comparison.

We've now come to the point in this book where it's appropriate to draw some conclusions from all of the chapters and illustrations of best practices that I have set out. The best way to draw those conclusions is to explore how all of these ideas can help you become a more effective and confident reviewer.

○ reducing appeals, grievances, and legal challenges

Let's begin with most reviewers' greatest fear: being taken to court because of an evaluation that they conducted. An old saying goes, "You can't prevent anyone from suing you, but you can prevent them from winning." When it comes to appeals, grievances, and legal challenges stemming from faculty reviews and evaluations, there's a great deal of truth in that sentiment. No matter how carefully you conduct a review, you can't prevent someone who receives a negative decision from appealing, filing a grievance, or entering into a lawsuit against you. But you can take steps that'll greatly reduce the likelihood that the person will be successful.

We saw the single most important action you can take in the first example of best practices we encountered in Chapter Two: *follow your institution's established procedures to the letter.* The courts are reluctant to intervene in situations where what is at issue is a matter of institutional standards. If Middling Passable University decides to tenure practically everyone, while Supercilious Prestigious University decides that no one's ever good enough to receive tenure, the courts will consider it a matter of institutional choice and academic freedom. But if one of those two colleges has a policy that says a professor's scholarly record consists of all the research he or she has ever done throughout his or her entire career, but a committee decides that only articles published within the last five years "count," the person who appeals is likely to find a sympathetic ear.

Internal appeal and grievance committees often work in the same way. People outside your discipline are often reluctant to overrule the standards set by an academic field. If a chemistry department decides that a faculty member's teaching was flawed because he or she repeatedly failed to instruct students in proper safety procedures, someone from the humanities is not likely to reject this conclusion because the instructor got good student evaluations. Similarly, if a music program decides that one of its faculty members' scholarship is weak because he or she hasn't performed off-campus in more than twenty years, an engineering faculty member will probably not oppose this conclusion because he or she really enjoyed one of this person's recitals. In short, appeals that find flaws in someone's adherence to established procedure are often successful. Those that relate to a discipline's own criteria often are not.

Related to the need to follow established policies is the need for a reasonable amount of consistency. If someone was promoted or tenured last year with certain credentials, and someone is denied this year with comparable credentials, there may well be grounds for a successful grievance. As we've already seen, however, it's certainly not the case that institutions or departments can't ratchet up their standards. It's not uncommon for institutions to have promoted someone to the rank of full professor twenty or thirty years ago with a portfolio that wouldn't even clear the minimum bar for tenure today. But gradual changes over the long term are different from what seem like sporadic changes from year to year designed simply to play favorites with one person and to punish or get rid of someone else. The key is to adopt a *reasonable* amount of consistency. Tightened standards should be phased in over time, with sufficient notice and opportunity for faculty members to meet them, and they should reflect the mission and vision of the discipline, college, and institution. At schools that have decided to change their role from teaching university to research university, increased requirements for research productivity make sense. At a teaching-focused community college, they probably don't—unless the institution was consistently following the principle that active researchers brought fresher ideas into their courses or something similar.

In two articles published in the winter and spring 2011 issues of *Department Chair*, Jon Dalager, dean of natural and social sciences at Wayne State College in Nebraska, outlined a number of other principles for avoiding pitfalls while conducting faculty reviews and evaluations. First, he cautions against many of the behaviors that distort the faculty rating process and cause problems for the reviewer when a decision is challenged:

- *Discrimination* by giving advantages to people the reviewer likes and withholding them from those he or she doesn't like.
- *Retaliation* by using the evaluation process to penalize a faculty member for something that is not clearly relevant to that particular evaluation.
- *Lack of advance preparation or mentoring* by failing to inform faculty members of the criteria and standards by which they'll be evaluated and thus setting them up for failure.
- *Insufficient record keeping* that makes it difficult or impossible to support the claims the reviewer is making. Maintaining records is particularly important in the case of evaluations in which the reviewer needs documentation that the faculty member can't or won't support. For instance, suppose during an annual evaluation that a department chair wishes to rate a faculty member as unsatisfactory in service because he or she consistently fails to attend meetings of committees or the department's faculty. But the faculty member submits an annual activity report that simply lists the number of committees on which he or she serves and a letter from one of the committee chairs thanking everyone who had been appointed to the group that year. Without minutes of meetings that indicate the faculty member was not present, statements from committee chairs noting their concerns, or even a log tracking the number of times the faculty member missed key events, the reviewer doesn't have the sort of evidence that can outweigh the faculty member's claims in the event of an appeal (Dalager, 2011a).

Dalager also notes that when faculty members appeal the result of an evaluation, they commonly do so on one or more of three grounds:

- The evaluation itself was flawed and missed key evidence.
- The evaluator's motivations were flawed.
- The faculty member's rights of academic freedom or nondiscrimination, or both, were violated.

Because these are such common bases for grievances and appeals, it's important for the reviewer to make certain that all protocols were followed in each of these areas. Was all the documentation supplied by the faculty member or required by the procedures thoroughly considered? Are there reasons why the reviewer can't provide—or can't be regarded as providing—a fair and impartial evaluation of this faculty member and thus should be recused? Has every care been taken to avoid even the appearance of discrimination, retaliation, or violation of internal procedures? "A department chair should conduct each evaluation as if it would be dissected by the courts," notes Dalager (2011b, p. 11). That advice holds equally well for other types of evaluations conducted by reviewers at other levels of the institution as well.

○ becoming more confident as a reviewer

Nevertheless, if you make it your goal merely not to get sued or to have a grievance filed against you when you conduct faculty evaluations, you're setting the bar far too low. What most reviewers want to do is to perform evaluations that are meaningful and helpful, recognize faculty members whose achievements have been commendable, enforce appropriate standards when work has been subpar, and help both their disciplines and institutions become better. That can be a rather demanding set of goals, particularly when you're relatively new to the process of evaluation and don't feel quite sure about what you're doing. So how can you improve your own skills as a reviewer while at the same time becoming more confident about these skills and less concerned about violating a policy or taking a step that's going to get either the institution or you into trouble? Here is some advice based on institutional best practices.

Excellent and confident reviewing comes with experience

To some extent, becoming better and less anxious as a reviewer simply takes time. The more reviews you conduct, the more familiar you'll be with applicable policies and the more comfortable you'll feel in your role as a reviewer. That advice may not seem helpful if this is your first stint conducting faculty evaluations and you haven't had an opportunity yet to gain the type of experience you feel you'll need.

You can take a shortcut to gain some experience through role-playing exercises with a mentor or colleague who has already been through this process a large number of times. Write drafts of several sample review letters—or complete the forms your institution uses—and have the other person examine them for phrases that could potentially cause problems or are unclear. Develop a few scenarios, and engage in some role playing as your colleague pretends to be the person you're reviewing, and you say the sorts of things you intend to say during an actual evaluation session.

This type of practice session will seem awkward at first, but if you go into it with the right attitude and have a colleague who supports your professional growth, it will soon begin to feel more natural. Remember that the point of the exercise isn't to give you experience in precisely what will happen in any particular review. Any set of documents submitted by a faculty member and any face-to-face session is going to be different from any other that you'll encounter. Rather, the point is to give you practice in selecting appropriate phrasing and responding to unexpected reactions. For this reason, it's probably best for your colleague not simply to accept what you say in either your written or oral mock evaluations but to try to surprise you with responses and objections that you wouldn't necessarily expect.

mini-case studies: role playing

For each of the following scenarios, imagine what you'd say in a written evaluation to the faculty member. Then envision a face-to-face meeting in which you'd discuss the result of your review with the faculty member. What would you say then?

o o o

You're conducting the annual evaluation of a distinguished full professor whose record of accomplishments vastly exceeds your own. Both at the institution and in your national disciplinary organization, this faculty member has already received every imaginable award. The past year has continued the professor's almost unbroken series of accomplishments, and your goal now is to report a highly positive result.

How do you accomplish this goal in a manner that's likely to be meaningful to the faculty member? What do you give the person who already has heard every accolade imaginable? How do you phrase your evaluation in a way that won't seem weak in light of the professor's life of achievements? You're in a situation similar to that of a student who doesn't want to call Hamlet "a well-written play" or Beethoven's Ninth Symphony "a good piece of music." How do you make your praise fresh and significant?

o o o

You've just concluded a tenure review of a faculty member your school has decided not to retain. The review committee has decided that although the person's teaching isn't awful, it's not distinctive or particularly effective either. In addition, the faculty member has clearly not met the research expectations of the discipline. This individual is frequently emotional and has had a habit of breaking into tears and becoming inconsolable at bad news.

How do you proceed with relating the results of the review?

o o o

You must terminate a faculty member because in the course of a posttenure review, you encountered allegations from several students of severe sexual harassment. You followed your institution's procedure for handling these cases, and the investigation resulted in a sufficient amount of credible evidence to regard the allegations as true. You have seen about a dozen e-mails that clearly violated the school's sexual harassment policy, as well as its policy on appropriate use of computer resources. This faculty member is hot-tempered and regularly lashes out at others when confronted with resistance.

How do you convey the results of this review?

o   o   o

You're the head of a review committee that's just evaluated a faculty member for promotion to full professor and denied that promotion by a very slim majority. The faculty member in question is likely to challenge you and become belligerent when presented with this decision. This person also thinks very quickly and is well known for having a fast, often compelling answer to justify his or her actions.

How do you relate to the faculty member this negative promotion decision?

Confidence comes from knowing how much support you have behind you

You'll be much more confident as a reviewer if you know that others in authority at your school back you up. Particularly if you're a relatively new reviewer, it can be useful to see whether your supervisor has roughly the same reaction to the faculty member's achievements that you do. As we saw in Chapter Three, in the case of negative decisions that affect someone's career or income, it can also be useful to have the office of human resources review the case with you. Staff members there can guide you in what you should and should not say, the sort of documentation that you'll need, and whether you have adequate grounds for your decision. It's natural to think of consulting your boss or the director of human resources when you're thinking of rendering a negative decision, but there are times when you may want their advice in more positive cases too. Particularly in situations where you haven't performed a lot of reviews or you're unsure about what your supervisor's views are on certain matters (perhaps because he or she is new to the position), there are benefits to be gained from discussing even positive cases with this person. After all, you don't want a positive recommendation at your level to be overturned at a higher level because you weren't aware of what standards that person would impose.

Similarly you don't want to be in the position of having made a promise to a faculty member because of his or her performance, only to discover that what you intended to do wasn't permissible under your institution's human resource policies. The only exception to the practice of checking with other offices in advance of releasing a review occurs when it's your supervisor or the office of human resources that must make the decision at the next level or hear any appeal that may be made, and that person feels uncomfortable discussing the faculty member's performance with you outside the prescribed process. In that case, you might ask the person for the name of someone who would be a suitable advisor or mentor to you as you formalize your decision. In other cases, if you know that the next levels of the institution are extremely likely to support your decision, you've followed all applicable policies, and you have appropriate grounds for the decision you're making, you'll be much more confident as the process unfolds.

Begin preparing for the evaluation far enough in advance

One of the most common reasons for not being confident in an evaluation is feeling that you're unprepared or may not have an answer for an objection the faculty member may raise. The best way to avoid this problem is to give yourself enough time to take all the steps you feel are necessary. Any review, no matter whether it's an annual evaluation of a faculty member who's obviously doing well or the most complex and politically charged tenure review imaginable, is something that the faculty member will take very seriously, and you need to do so as well.

Plot out on your calendar the steps that'll be necessary to complete each stage of the process and block out sufficient time for them. In years when you have a particularly large number of reviews to make, adjust your calendar accordingly so that you won't need to shortchange any candidate. Remember that last-minute complications can always occur, so build in even more time than you believe you'll need. If these blocks of time aren't fixed on your calendar, appointments and meetings will soon arise and consume all the opportunities you thought you'd have.

Particularly in systems where faculty members submit multiple binders of material, it can be extraordinarily time-consuming to gain even passing familiarity with the items provided for you to review. You don't want to make a judgment that you may well not have made if you'd only taken a bit more time to examine all the evidence. Knowing that you've been thorough, given yourself the chance to consider carefully what you'll say and why, and allowed yourself an opportunity for serious second thoughts is the best confidence builder you can have.

general conclusion and final advice

There are plenty of resources available if you would like to develop your skills in conducting faculty reviews and evaluations even further. A number of administrative training programs—such as the Kansas State University Academic Chairpersons Conference held each February (http://www.dce.k-state.edu/conf/academicchairpersons/), and the IDEA Center's Department Chair Seminars (http://www.theideacenter.org/category/our-services/department-chair-seminars)—regularly offer sessions explicitly devoted to best practices in conducting reviews. At the dean's level, the Council of Colleges of Arts and Sciences (http://www.ccas.net/i4a/pages/index.cfm?pageid=1) often addresses topics related to reviews and evaluations at its annual conference or in its workshops. Webinars on various aspects of academic administration are offered by such organizations as the American Council on Education (http://www.acenet.edu/AM/Template. cfm?Section=ACE_Webinar_Series&TEMPLATE=/CM/ HTMLDisplay.cfm&CONTENTID=42544), Jossey-Bass (http://www. departmentchairs.org/online-training.aspx), Magna Publications (http://www.magnapubs.com/online/seminars/), and Innovative Educators (http://www.innovativeeducators.org/webinars_s/82.htm).

Although topics vary each year, it's a good idea to keep an eye on the issues that these webinars will address since conducting evaluations effectively is a central part of sound higher education administration. Although it can be a bit more expensive, another choice is to bring one or more consultants specializing in faculty reviews and evaluations to your campus in order to provide a training program designed for your institution's needs or to coach individual administrators in more effective evaluation techniques. These services are available from a wide range of providers, including the IDEA Center (http:// www.theideacenter.org/helpful-resources/consulting-general/00143-consulting-services), ATLAS: Academic Training, Leadership, and Assessment Services (www.atlasleadership.com), and the two internationally recognized experts in faculty evaluation whose work we considered in Chapters Ten and Eleven, Raoul Arreola (rarreola @utmem.edu) and Peter Seldin (pseldin@pace.edu).

Finally, I end this book with the single best piece of advice any academic leader can receive:

---

the best practice of all

If you approach every evaluation by asking, "How would I want to be treated if I were receiving this review?" you will almost always make the wisest possible decision.

References

Dalager, J. K. (2011a). Legal issues in faculty evaluation: Avoiding problems. *Department Chair, 23*(3), 9–11.

Dalager, J. K. (2011b). Legal issues in faculty evaluation: When evaluations go bad. *Department Chair, 23*(4), 10–11.

index

Page references followed by *fig* indicate an illustrated figure, followed by *t* indicate a table.

A

The Academic Portfolio (Seldin and Miller), 215
Academically Adrift (Arum and Roksa), 9
Accountability: higher education trends leading to demands for, 6–9; posttenure review driven by demand for, 109. *See also* Faculty evaluation
Accountability culture: higher education trends leading to, 6–9; significance for reviewers, 10–17
Adam, B. E., 138
Adams, C. L., 138
Addison, W. E., 39
The Administrative Portfolio (Seldin and Higgerson), 215
Albers, C., 138
Aleamoni, L. M., 39, 193
Almodovar, Jimenez v., 155
Amacher, R. C., 155
Amano, I., 3
American Association of University Professors (AAUP): academic tenure promoted by, 154; on communicating negative tenure decision, 168; Declaration of Principles (1915) of, 152–153; four strategies on tenure decisions, 161–162; regarding posttenure review, 110; Statement of Principles on Academic Freedom and Tenure (1940) of, 153; "unethical conduct" ground for tenure revocation based on statement of, 156
American Council on Education, 162, 168, 246
Anger: don't respond with, 122; don't use logic to overcome, 122; handling posttenure review, 120–123; options for dealing with denial and, 101–103

Annual goals: evaluating progress on, 80–82; mini-case studies on evaluating progress of, 81–82; mini-case studies on setting, 79; setting new, 78–79
Annual performance appraisals: evaluating progress on annual goals, 80–82; formative-summative, 82–84; four key steps to follow for all, 86; given when major issues arise, 85–86; offering constructive criticism during, 68–73; offering praise and recognition during, 74–77; setting new annual goals during, 78–79; for the staff, 84–85; understanding difference between annual and overall progress, 71; wide-spread institutional use of, 67–68
Apologies, 122
Appeals: behaviors that can be cause of, 239; best practices for reducing, 237–240; common grounds for, 240
Appraisals: annual performance, 67–87; description of, 15, 68
Armstrong Atlantic State University, 143
Arreola model: adapted to individual institution needs and culture, 194; advantages and disadvantages of the, 205–206; using appropriate sources about scholarship, 200–203; core composite indicators derived from, 210*t*; creating an integrated approach by borrowing from the, 230, 231–232*fig*, 233–234*fig*; effectiveness at emphasizing most important factors, 34; eight-step process of, 193–194; identifying and using mechanisms for obtaining needed information, 203–204; mini-case studies on using the, 209–211*t*, 212*t*–213*t*; objectivity advantage of, 199, 229;

249

index

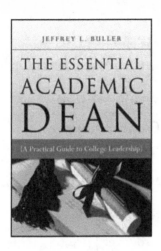

The Essential
Academic Dean

*A Practical Guide to
College Leadership*

Jeffrey L. Buller

ISBN 978-0-470-18086-0

Paperback | p 448

The role of an academic dean is extremely complex, involving budgeting, community relations, personnel decisions, managing a large enterprise, mastering numerous details, fundraising, and guiding a school or college toward a compelling vision for the future. But no academic dean can quickly master all of the intricacies involved in this challenging position. For instance, how do you build support for a shared vision of your unit's future? How do you interact effectively with all of the different internal and external constituencies that a dean must serve? How do you set, supervise, and implement a budget? How do you handle the volume of documents that cross your desk? How do you fire someone, ask a chair to step down, respond to a reporter on the telephone, and settle disputes about intellectual property rights? How do you know when it's time to consider leaving your current position for another opportunity?

The Essential Academic Dean is about the "how" of academic leadership. Based on a series of workshops given by the author on college administration and management, each topic deals concisely with the most important information deans need at their fingertips when faced with a particular challenge or opportunity. Written both as a comprehensive guide to the academic deanship and as a ready reference to be consulted when needed, this book emphasizes proven solutions over untested theories and stresses what deans need to know now in order to be most successful as academic leaders.

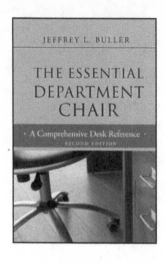

The Essential
Department Chair

Second Edition

A Comprehensive Desk Reference

Jeffrey L. Buller

ISBN 978-1-118-12374-4

Hardcover | p 496

This second edition of the informative and influential *The Essential Department Chair* offers academic chairs and department heads the information they need to excel in their roles. This book is about the "how" of academic administration: for instance, how do you cultivate a potential donor for much-needed departmental resources? How do you persuade your department members to work together more harmoniously? How do you keep the people who report to you motivated and capable of seeing the big picture?

Thoroughly revised, updated, and expanded, this classic resource covers a broad spectrum of timely topics and is now truly more than a guide—it's a comprehensive desk reference that tells you "everything you need to know to be a department chair." *The Essential Department Chair* contains information on topics such as essentials of creating a strategic plan, developing and overseeing a budget, key elements of fundraising, preparing for the role of chair, meeting the challenges of mentoring to increase productivity, and creating a more collegial atmosphere. The book also explores the chair's role in the search process, how to conduct a successful interview, and what to do when it's time to let someone go. The author includes suggestions for the best practices to adopt when doing an evaluation or assessment, and a wealth of new case studies to equip leaders in this pivotal position to excel in departmental and institutional life.